Tours of Okinawa

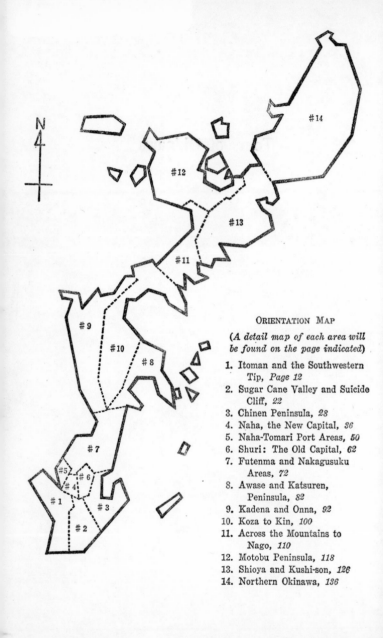

N

ORIENTATION MAP

(A detail map of each area will be found on the page indicated)

Tours of
Okinawa
A Souvenir Guide
to Places of Interest

COMPILED BY Isamu Fuchaku, Gasei Higa,
AND Zenkichi Toyama UNDER THE
AUSPICES OF U.S. ARMY SPECIAL SERVICE
CLUBS OKINAWA

ILLUSTRATED BY Gasei Higa

CHARLES E. TUTTLE COMPANY
Rutland, Vermont & Tokyo, Japan

Representatives
Continental Europe: BOXERBOOKS, INC., *Zurich*
British Isles: PRENTICE-HALL INTERNATIONAL, INC., *London*
Australasia: PAUL FLESCH & CO., PTY. LTD., *Melbourne*
Canada: M. G. HURTIG LTD., *Edmonton*

Published by the
Charles E. Tuttle Company, Inc.
of Rutland, Vermont and Tokyo, Japan
with editorial offices at
Suido 1-chome, 2-6, Bunkyo-ku, Tokyo

Library of Congress
Catalog Card No. 59-14086

International Standard Book No. 0-8048-0594-6

First edition, 1959
Eighth printing, 1971

Printed in Japan

Table
of
Contents

Foreword

Many questions have been asked by those who have gone on Service Club Tours with us, and in an effort to answer these we produced last year, in mimeographed form, a booklet entitled *Tours of Okinawa*. Besides answering those many questions we hoped it would provide a supplement to the trips enjoyed and the pictures taken which may be kept as a reminder of the places, the people, the history, and the culture of Okinawa. We are glad to say that the popularity of the booklet and the present demand for further copies of it has made it possible to reproduce it in more permanent form.

As in the former booklet there are route maps and sketches, which have been redrawn for this new edition. The text material is the same, having been compiled from a number of previous publications listed in the bibliography. As such it may seem trite as information; but our purpose has been to relate this information to a series of planned tours and to correlate the material on history and culture with the places on particular routes. A further purpose has been to introduce several lesser known places that can be found along, or diverging from, the routes between better-publicized places of interest. This increases the number of separate tours which may be scheduled.

We wish to express our thanks here to those who helped us compile the original booklet without which this first edition would not have been produced. We are indebted to Miss Emily May Harper of Army Service Club No. 1, Sukiran, for guidance and supervision in compiling the information and planning materials for the original booklet; to Pfc. Norbert E. Brauner, a pleasant companion and efficient driver on reconnaissance trips made to determine routes and site locations; to our co-workers who assisted in various ways, often assuming some of our regular tasks while we were engaged on this project; and last, but far from least, to the USARYIS, Special Services Section, without whose backing this book would still remain a partial thought rather than the finished work we now may offer you, our reader.

Isamu Fuchaku, ASC No. 1—Sukiran
Zenkichi Toyama, ASC No. 2—Naha
Gasei Higa, ASC No. 1—Sukiran

Itoman and the South-western Tip

Itoman   This is one of the largest fishing villages on Okinawa. It is located 12 kilometers to the southwest of Naha; and in olden times was a part of the area called Kanegusuku. It was established as a separate town in 1908. Developed on an inclined, raised coral reef, it has a population of nearly 14,000, and an area of 1.8 kilometers. Although a part of the population is engaged in agriculture, and industrial and commercial pursuits, a majority of the males are fishermen. They, at the risk of their lives, have for many years made voyages in canoes 8 meters long and 1 meter wide to many parts of the Ryukyus, and also to Japan and the South Sea Islands, giving full scope to their ability as fishermen. As the husbands of the town are frequently away from their homes for long periods, the housewives of Itoman have to manage all the domestic and community affairs such as finance, public relations, and the education of their children. They are reputed to be healthy, industrious, economical, and chaste. In Itoman, the women have a position unique in oriental countries; they enjoy equal rights with men and are financially independent. When the fisher-husband returns from his sailing, the wife buys his catch from him and sells it at the market for what profit she can obtain. They have an arrangement between them for the mutual support of the household and children. The famous annual event in Itoman is the *Haryusen,* boat races between three teams of

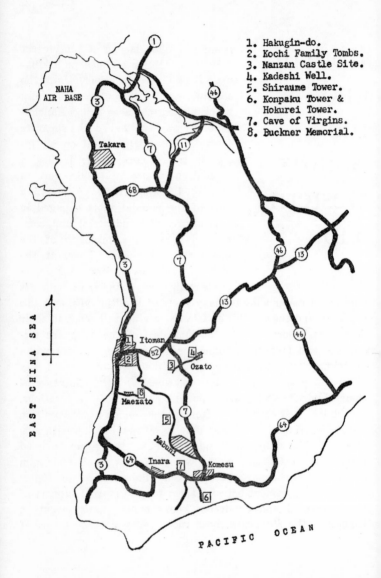

1. Hakugin-do.
2. Kochi Family Tombs.
3. Nanzan Castle Site.
4. Kadeshi Well.
5. Shiraume Tower.
6. Konpaku Tower &
   Hokurei Tower.
7. Cave of Virgins.
8. Buckner Memorial.

townsfolk, which is held on the fourth of May in the lunar calendar. At this festival, those fishermen who have been missing since the last year's celebration are declared legally dead and the wives become officially widows.

The Itoman area was the scene of final Japanese resistance in the Battle of Okinawa. Their last stronghold was the escarpment running east from Itoman called Yaeju Dake. A number of war memorials add to tourist interest in this area.

Hakugindo Shrine   Here the only tutelary god of Itoman is enshrined; it is situated at the north entrance to the town and is well respected by the townsfolk. According to tradition, the king's young wife went daily to the marker at the shrine to pray for a son and her prayers were answered. Today it is the custom for all new wives to go to this shrine and pray for sons. In 1933 an impressive shrine was erected by donations of the townspeople, but it was destroyed in the last war. The present building, built since the war with contributions from the citizens of Itoman, is a picturesque one standing on a low wooded hill.

Kochi Family Tombs   This tomb, the largest family tomb on Okinawa, is an unusual structure. Four smaller tombs form a line in front of a larger tomb. The smaller tombs belong to separate branches of the family; the large tomb is the permanent burial place for all branches of the family and includes several generations. When death occurs in a branch of the family, the body is placed in one of the smaller tombs. After three years, the bones are removed to the large family (or clan) tomb. However, if any member of the family lives to be 80 or more years old, he is buried

HAKUGINDO SHRINE

immediately in the large tomb. This is in recognition of the honor which such long life of any member bestows upon the entire family. If any member has brought dishonor to the family, his body is not placed in the family tomb; it is buried outside the wall enclosing the tomb, to the right of the entrance.

Buckner   A snub-nosed monument on the tip of a high
Memorial   hill about a mile and a half north from the
               fishing village of Itoman marks the site where
the leader of the ground forces in the Battle of Okinawa, General Simon Bolivar Buckner, was killed on June 18, 1945. The Japanese were entrenched in their last stronghold and

CAVE OF THE VIRGINS

General Buckner was watching the progress of the fighting on this southwestern tip of the island. A Japanese dual purpose gun across the valley spotted his movement and zeroed in on the area with a hail of projectiles which scattered debris in every direction. Buckner was struck in the chest by a jagged piece of coral and died ten minutes later. Four days after his death, organized resistance on Okinawa came to an end. Buckner and 7,000 of his soldier and marine comrades had fallen on this island that was no more than a dot on the world map. Buckner had led them through 88 days of the bitterest, most costly battle of World War II. The weather has worn the granite surface of the monument near Itoman, but his

memory is also preserved in facets of American living on Okinawa. The post is called "Fort Buckner"; the cove at the south
end of Nakagusuku Wan on the Pacific Coast is "Buckner Bay".

Cave   The name of this monument is actually "Himeyuri-
of   no-To" (Lilly Tower). It is located 300 meters
the   east of E-baru, Miwa-son, and is a memorial to
Virgins   the souls of 143 students of Okinawa First Girls'
             High School and their 15 teachers. They had
joined the Japanese Army as volunteer nurses on the U.S.
invasion of Okinawa and were, together with Japanese soldiers,
chased up to this cave, where a Japanese Army Field Hospital
was located. Various accounts explain how the girls were
killed. The generally accepted one is that, in the mopping up
process, a Nisei American soldier, not knowing who was in the
cave, called out in Japanese for the occupants to surrender.
When there was no reply after several warnings, the cave was
neutralized with flame throwers and demolition charges.

Hokurei   One of two memorials to the unknown dead of
Tower   World War II, this tower is located about 500
             meters south of Komesu, Miwa-son. It was erected
under the auspices of the Hokkaido Prefecture Government
Bereaved Families Association and the *Hokkaido Times* newspaper to the memory of 10,000 Hokkaido-born soldiers who
were killed in the Okinawan campaign. In April 1954, 25
representatives of the soldiers' families in Hokkaido visited
this site for the dedication ceremonies.

Kompaku   This is the other unknown warriors' monument
Tower   at this site where a fierce and desperate battle

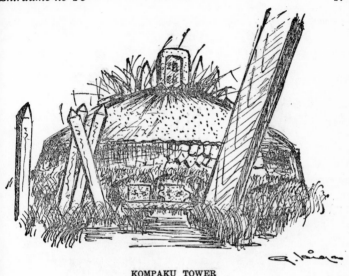

KOMPAKU TOWER

put an end to the hard-fought Okinawa campaign. It was erected to the souls of the Japanese soldiers and the Okinawan monument was the gift of the villagers of Mawashi immediately after the war when the people had very little money. So the tower is not an elegant column, but its poor state provokes a sadness for those it honors and a gratitude to those who provided this token to their memory.

Shiraume-
no-To
Located East of Kunishi Village is another World War II memorial. It is dedicated to the souls of the 74 Okinawa Second Girls' High School students and their 11 teachers. They had joined the Japanese Army as volunteer nurses and ended their young

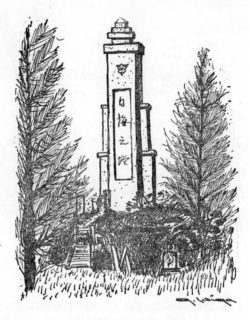

SHIRAUME-NO-TO

lives by suicide when the American advance made Japanese surrender imminent. The monument stands on top of the cave where the young women died. *Shiraume* means "white plum."

Nanzan   This castle dates from about 1301 when Okinawa
Castle   was under the misrule of the sensuous young king,
           Tamagusuku, whose feudal lords revolted against him and brought about the collapse of the united kingdom, establishing in its stead the North, South, and Middle Kingdoms.   The South came under the rule of Nanzan, who built

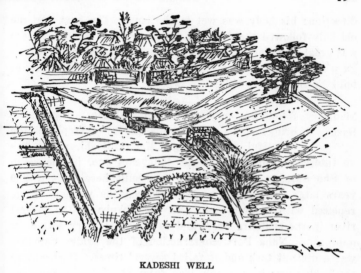

KADESHI WELL

this castle. War continued among the three kingdoms for over 100 years until the ruler of the Middle Kingdom defeated the northern ruler in 1416 and the southern ruler in 1429, re-uniting Okinawa. The castle was destroyed in feudal wars; today only a tomb and a stone marker remain.

Kadeshi Well   This is located in Ozato Village, east of Nanzan Castle. It was built in three sections; a drinking water section, a bathing section, and a laundry section. Although used for hundreds of years, the source of the water supply has never run dry. According to tradition, about 800 years ago, there was a severe and prolonged drought and the people of this area were faced with starvation. One day an old lady found her dog coming home from the eastern

direction; his body was wet to the bone. The next day the
old lady followed the dog and discovered this spring. There
was great rejoicing among the people, who named it Kariyushi-
ga which means "Happy Spring." The wells and baths were
built by the townspeople.

Madan   About 2 kilometers east of Naha, a postwar steel
Bashi   bridge spans the Kokuba River; it replaces the
            beautiful stone bridge, Madan Bashi, which has
an interesting history. About 450 years ago, in the reign
of Sho Shin, a wooden bridge was built here. About 200
years later the ruler, Sho Tei, ordered the wooden bridge
replaced with a stone one. As the Kokuba is the largest
river in the southern area, and as its bed is very soft as it
approaches Naha Port, construction of the bridge supports
was a difficult task and it failed several times. However, as
the bridge was on the only way from Shuri to the southern
castle, it was important to the king who issued a mandate that
it must be completed. A total of 9,000 masons and 83,000
laborers from villages throughout Okinawa worked on the
project. It was finally completed at the cost of the life of a
woman "with seven colors in her hair" who was buried under
the stone base of the bridge. The story of the woman's
sacrifice and of the romance, years later, between her beautiful
daughter and a young prince of Shuri is incorporated in a
popular Ryukyuan folk drama, *The Building of Madan Bashi*.

The beautiful stone bridge was 360 feet long and was
greatly admired for its beauty, which was achieved by the
skillful use of lines without any additional decoration. It was
totally destroyed in World War II.

Sugar Cane Valley and Suicide Cliff

This tour approaches Suicide Cliff via Route 46 which traverses the heart of what might be called "Sugar Cane Valley". Statistics show that 310 *chobu* (over 700 acres) in this area are planted in sugar cane, feeding the Ryukyus Sugar Company Mill— a lone representative of industry in this rural, agricultural community. Since prewar times, this section has been a prosperous farming area producing sugar and textiles.

During World War II, there was a Japanese army hospital in this valley. As the Japanese retreated toward Suicide Cliff, they were obliged to leave an estimated 2000 sick and wounded who perished here. A commemorative stone has been placed at the spot where their bones were found, but the site has not been cared for and the stone is almost obscured by weeds.

Suicide Cliff   Memorable as a site of wartime tragedy, this cliff stands on the sea-ward side of Mount Mabuni, a promontory of the Yaeju Dake escarpment which runs east from Itoman. Here the Japanese Army had prepared their final defenses in the Okinawa campaign, establishing their Headquarters in a cave on the side of the mountain. There are three war memorials located in this area: Shimamori-no-To, Reimei-no-To, and Kenji-no-To. They remind Okinawans of the time when their little island country was the scene of some of the fiercest battles of the Pacific War.

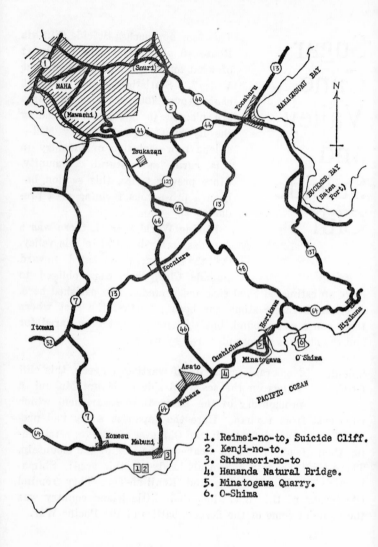

1. Reimei-no-to, Suicide Cliff.
2. Kenji-no-to.
3. Shimamori-no-to
4. Hananda Natural Bridge.
5. Minatogawa Quarry.
6. O-Shima

Reimei-
no-To
This monument is located at the top of Mount Mabuni in Miwa-son. It is the site where Lt. Gen. Mitsuru Ushijima, Commanding General of the 32nd Japanese Army, and his staff officer, General Isamu Cho, committed harakiri. They had fought a desperate battle during the 80 days since the United States forces invaded Okinawa on the first of April 1945. Despite his strategies, which have been termed the best Japanese defense in the Pacific war, he was unable to turn the tide of war, and had withdrawn to this corner of the island. On the 19th of June, the General issued an order to all the army units to "Fight to the last, and die for the Eternal Cause!" At the same time, he sent a farewell telegram to the Minister of War in Tokyo. At 4:30 A.M. on the 23rd of June, when the moon was about to set in the South Sea, he and his staff officer put an end to their own lives after the old samurai fashion. Their remains were buried at this site by U.S. soldiers. The present monument was built by a group of Japanese contractors headed by a Mr. Niimura and dedicated in June 1952 by the Okinawan priest, Nako, from the Gokoku-ji (a temple) at Nami-no-ue.

Kenji-
no-To
On the 31st of March 1945, all the students of the Okinawa Normal School were recruited and formed into the "Normal School Students' Troop". The troop consisted of a headquarters, a *Kirikomi Tai* or Attack Squad, *Chihaya Tai*, or the Field Fortification Company, and a Special Forces Company. On April 1, they began to take part in the action. The 500 student troops fought bravely in one place after another under the shower of bullets, but two-thirds of them had been killed when they reached the cliff-side of Mabuni on the 19th of June. Some took part in

the suicidal attack here and others killed themselves. This monument located in the cave at the foot of the cliff is sacred to the memory of the 18 teachers, headed by their principal, Mr. Noda, and the 289 students who were killed during the last battle.

The bones of other Japanese soldiers who were killed or committed suicide at this last point of organized resistance may be seen here. A considerable portion of these have been carried away by morbid minded souvenir hunters; the remaining few have been placed behind a cement wall.

Shimamori-   Located east of Mabuni Hill is a monument to
no-To   Mr. Shimada, war-time Governor of Okinawa,
                 Mr. Arai, Director of the Police Department,
and about 380 members of the Okinawa Prefectural Government staff. Mr. Shimada had, on his coming to the island for his new post, occupied himself with the difficult task of wartime administration: resettlement of the people as the war uprooted them, securing of foodstuffs, and cooperation with military policies. He and his staff had moved south with the military in the effort to keep a semblance of civil administration among the people. It is believed that Governor Shimada was killed on this spot at about the same time that Commander Ushijima committed suicide. Construction of this monument was started in March of 1951 with donations from the general public and the former personnel of the Prefectural Government. The unveiling ceremony was held on 25 June 1951 with the Governor's widow, Mrs. Shimada, attending. She came down from Tokyo.

For the return from Suicide Cliff the way along the coast

KENJI-NO-TO

to O-Shima and turning north on Route 48 is suggested after a visit to this small offshore island. About 1¼ miles southeast of the coastal village of Asato there is a fresh-water spring which tumbles from the low seaside cliffs. It is called Keiza Waterfall and is presently being sought by the city of Naha as a source for augmenting its inadequate water supply.

Hananda Natural Bridge
In Gushichan village there is a large hole in the rock through which the Yokota River flows. It seems that the resulting natural bridge was the result of erosion over many years by the rapid

stream of the Yokota River. The shrub-encrusted natural
formation is admired by many visitors.

Also in Gushichan there is an example of the natural spring
well usually associated with Kin Village. The well in Gushichan is called Yaguso-ga and the story of its discovery during
a drought is quite similar to the one told of the Kadeshi well
in the Itoman tour.

Minatogawa   The stone produced from the Minatogawa
Quarry   Quarry is very popular as a building material.
               It is similar to our Travertine and is called
awa ishi (bubble stone). It is easy to carve, increases in
hardness on exposure to the air, and is used extensively for
the building of school houses, warehouses, and retaining walls.
The stones are usually cut from the quarry in blocks 1 foot
by 3 feet by 8 inches or the larger 1 foot by 1 foot by six feet
size. There are almost inexhaustible resources in the quarry,
but production methods are so slow that there is not enough
cut stone produced to fulfil the demand. About one hundred
people work in the quarry each day earning a total of about
6,000,000 yen per annum. The "Dragon's Roost", USARYIS
Teen Club in the Plaza area, is built of this type of stone.

Shiranga   These falls form a natural lake in the Gushichan
Falls   area which has been used to make an irrigation
              system for rice paddies in this section. Funds
for construction of the sluice-ways were provided by GRI in
1952.

O-shima   A small islet lies just about 600 feet offshore
              from Kudeken village. There is only one village

KANNON-DO ON O-SHIMA

on the island. For a long time the villagers suffered with the inconvenience of a ferry boat to the mainland. They had used village funds at three separate times to build a bridge, but each in succession was destroyed by war and typhoon. Government funds were finally secured in 1952 to build a concrete bridge. The bridge which cost 4,018,000 yen to build was opened in June 1953. There is a Kannon-do, or temple of Kannon on the island, about 500 feet from the bridge. It is not clear just when the temple was built, but it is considered to be quite old. It is well respected by the villagers, and contains a few old stone carvings that will be of interest to the visitor.

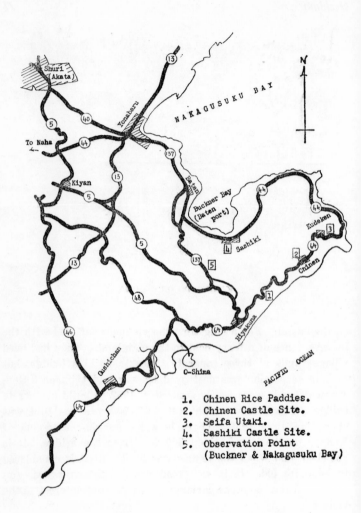

1. Chinen Rice Paddies.
2. Chinen Castle Site.
3. Seifa Utaki.
4. Sashiki Castle Site.
5. Observation Point
   (Buckner & Nakagusuku Bay)

Chinen Peninsula

For this tour, we suggest taking Routes 5, 13, and 48 to Route 64, thus going around the Chinen Peninsula from the south as the view is much more scenic this way with the ocean on your right.

Sugar Cane Fields. Along Routes 5 and 13, fields of tall plants will be seen in many places; these are the sugar cane plants; black cake sugar and white powdered sugar are produced from them. No date is given for the first cultivation of sugar cane on Okinawa, but the plant is known to have been imported from China through Japan. The plant was cultivated in the time of King Sho-Ho (1622 to 1642), but up to that time had only been used in the raw form. In 1623, a man named Gima Shinjo learned sugar refining in China and returned to circulate the techniques of manufacture throughout Okinawa. The refined product was only used to pay the tribute which the king of Okinawa sent to Japan, and cultivation of sugar cane was limited by the government to acreage just sufficient to produce the tribute amount. In 1889 the government (by this time Japanese) cancelled the limitations on sugar cultivation and acreage increased throughout the island. Today sugar is an important export of the Ryukyus.

Chinen Rice Paddies Chinen was the cradle of rice culture in the Ryukyus. As you start north on Highway 64 and pass the village of Hiyakuna, extensive fields of rice spread along the seashore to the east. The green paddies, combined with a beautiful coast-line and adjacent small islands rising above the blue water, make the sight wonderful enough to persuade you to stop and admire the beauties of nature.   Leading to the beach, there is a road that can be traveled by car.   At low tide you can walk to some of the nearer small islands.

Chinen   This castle stood on a hill in Chinen village about
Castle   100 yards from Highway 64.   According to tradi-
Site   tion, the god who created the Ryukyu Islands
           came to this site from Kudaka Island to worship
here.   Each successive king of the Chinen area made his castle on this site.   The castle was called "Chinen Bandokoro", "Guard over the Land".   This castle was in fair state of pres- ervation until 1900; but today, only the main stone gate, the west gate, and a portion of the wall remain.   The castle site is designated as a valuable treasure of the Ryukyus by the Cultural Property Protection Commission.

Seifa   is closely associated with the mythological origin
Utaki   of the Ryukyus.   According to this belief, the
           god who created the world first descended to Kudaka
Island, some five miles due east from here, and later migrated to Okinawa Island.   In the early days the king came to this spot to worship the gods, bowing in the direction of Kudaka Island.   An important festival was also held at this place. It was called "Ura Uri" which can be roughly translated as "First Descent".   This ceremony was concerned with the ancient Ryukyuan religion and commemorated the inaugura- tion of each new *Kikoe Ogimi* or High Priestess of the realm. This important post was traditionally held by a sister of the king.   The ceremony, which was held at night, invariably

CHINEN CASTLE SITE

attracted great crowds of people. Priestesses gathered here for the festival from all parts of the kingdom; those from Kudaka Island brought with them the sacred objects which were symbolic of the mythological origin of the world and which, at all other times, remained enshrined in their temple.

Tsukishiro-no-Miya   Located in Sashiki Village, this is the place where King Sho-Hashi lived until he was 33 years old and before he was finally made king to rule over all the islands. The shrine standing here was built by the succeeding generation of Sho kings (1440-1445) and dedicated to his memory and to the accomplishments of

his 18-year reign (1422-1440). There were once the extensive
buildings of Sashiki Castle on this site, but now scarcely a
trace of even the wall is to be found. This is because the
stones of the castle and its walls are believed to have been
moved by Sho-Hashi to Shuri to build a castle for himself
there when he became king.

View
Over
Nakagusuku
Bay

From the hill of Shinzato village on Route
137 there is an impressive view of the southeast coast of Okinawa along Nakagusuku
Bay. On the right, a part of the Chinen
Peninsula sticks out into the sea and the high
Shukuna Mountain can be seen. Away to the north, Katsuren
Peninsula juts out making the north end of the bay; Tsuken
and Hamahija Islands float like gems in the waters near it.
Along the coast between Chinen and Katsuren are fields of
sugar cane, sweet potatoes, and rice with pine forests framing
them on the rugged hills which rise from the coast, the highest
being the site of the famous Nakagusuku Castle.

Immediately below, the village of Baten spreads along the
sea. Baten is the second largest village in the Chinen area
and has long been a center of shipping, shipbuilding, basket
weaving, and tile making. The sheltered cove on which the
village of Baten is located was formerly known as Baten Port,
but has been renamed Buckner Bay in honor of General Simon
Bolivar Buckner. This cove and the area of Nakagusuku Bay
near it were used as a military port in World War II and
many large warships were anchored here. To-day there are
only a few fishing vessels; the many damaged ships which
cluttered the bay following the war have been removed by
salvage operations.

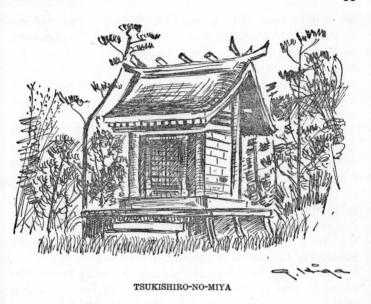

TSUKISHIRO-NO-MIYA

Further up Route 137, at the very crest of the hill, the offices and billets of American Military Government for Okinawa were located in the years immediately following World War II. This was then a popular route of travel for Americans who called the lofty site of their operations "Top of the Rock".

Yonabaru-cho   This is the largest town in the Chinen-Tamagusuku-Sashiki district. Located about six miles east of Naha on Nakagusuku Bay, it had a population in 1956 of 7,318 persons in 1,501 families. Prior to 1949, Yonabaru was a part of the farming district of Ozato-

son, but in April of that year it became an independent *cho*
(town). It is a trading center for fishing and agricultural
products. Its beautiful, sandy beaches are rated among the
best on the island; the waters of the bay are as calm as an
inland sea, and swimming here is a popular recreation. Two
important buildings in the town are the Chinen High School
and the Yonabaru Power Company.

Yonabaru has always been the trade and traffic center of
the southeast coast; and, until 1945, it was an important
railroad junction. There was a narrow gauge steam railroad
from here to Naha and a horse-drawn rail coach to the village
of Awase. There was regular steamship travel from Yonabaru
to Kunigami and Higashi-son in northern Okinawa and to
Amami O-Shima, Japan. The breakwater and sea-wall of
the port were damaged in World War II and the port became
too shallow for vessels of any size.

Yonabaru has long been famous for its annual Tug-of-War
which is held on the 26th of June in the lunar calendar.
Throngs of people come from far and near to watch a crowd
almost as large tugging the enormous hemp rope along the
seashore like so many ants carrying a long earthworm. The
origin of this festival is obscure; even the old people of the
town have no definite memory of its history. Some say it is
a harvest festival of thanks; others say that it is a petition for
water. One historian says that, about 400 years ago, the
village had a water shortage about this time of the year and
the people gathered to pray for rain; this may have been how
the festival was initiated. But whether to petition or to
thank, they still gather each year for this celebration which
has become almost synonymous with the name of their town.

Naha, the New Capital

Five hundred years ago, Naha was only a poor village on an isolated islet in the estuary of the Kokuba River. Today it is a bustling metropolis with an area of approximately 2,150 acres and a population of 200,000. According to the 1958 census, about one fourth the total population of the Ryukyu Islands lives in the four districts (Oroku, Tsuboya, Mawashi, and Shuri) which are now incorporated as Naha Shi (city). The development of the city, in many ways, parallels that of cities in the United States—a pattern of new social, political, industrial, and commercial interests attracting increasingly more people. The city is now gradually enveloping its suburbs.

The early Naha developed rapidly after King Sho-Kimfuku (1450-1454) had the Chokotei dyke constructed to deepen the port and the bulk of foreign trade moved from Tomari to Naha Port. In the Old Dynasty Era (before 1470), Naha was a commercial-industrial city consisting of four towns (Nishi, Higashi, Izumizaki, and Wakasa) and the two villages of Kumoji and Tomari. When the Japanese placed the administration of the Ryukyus under the Home Office at Tokyo in 1874 and reduced the king of Okinawa to a marquis of Japan in 1879, Naha replaced Shuri as the capital city. In 1903, the Kainohama district of Oroku and the Makishi district of Mawashi became a part of Naha Shi. The city continued to develop until its area spread over Jogoku, Tsuboya, and Ameku.

Prior to World War II, Naha was the center of politics,

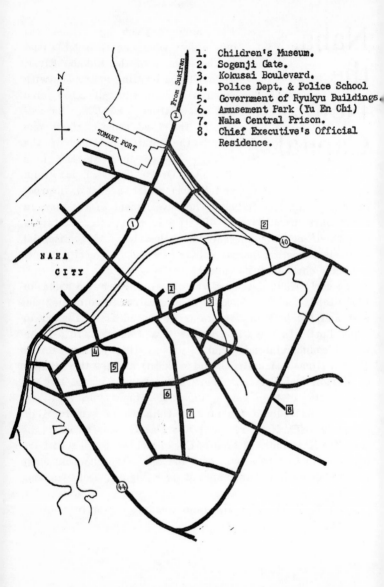

1. Children's Museum.
2. Sogenji Gate.
3. Kokusai Boulevard.
4. Police Dept. & Police School
5. Government of Ryukyu Buildings.
6. Amusement Park (Yu En Chi)
7. Naha Central Prison.
8. Chief Executive's Official Residence.

economy, and education. Government agencies, newspaper companies, banks, commercial firms, hotels, hospitals, temples and shrines were concentrated here. Three narrow gauge railroads transported passengers and produce from its terminal to Itoman, Yonabaru, and Kadena. By 1944, the population of the city proper was over 60,000 with another 20,000 living in its adjoining suburbs. Naha was a prosperous and valuable asset to Japan as she emerged from the Meiji restoration to become a world power, and was the first object of retaliation by Japan's enemies in the battle of Okinawa. On 10 October 1944, the age-old city was completely demolished in a severe bombing raid by carrier based planes of the United States. It was further devastated as the battle moved through the city to its conclusion on the hills south of Oroku.

From 1945 to 1951, the areas west of Kokusai-Makishi Boulevard (today's main street) were largely occupied by U.S. military units. For this reason, residential resettlement and commercial rebuilding was relegated to the Tsuboya area which became the "City Center" with stores, markets, restaurants, hotels, and movie houses mushrooming in this section. The area was low, poorly drained, and relatively unattractive to investment before the war; with the rebuilding, land values here increased 100%.

The United States Administration and the Ryukyuan Government moved to Naha in 1949, making their offices in a school building in the Nami-no-ue area which had survived the war sufficiently to be restored for this purpose. In the same year, Minato-mura was incorporated into the city, increasing the population beyond the prewar figure; and the evacuation of troop units from this area began.

A city plan for a greater Naha-shi was inaugurated in 1949

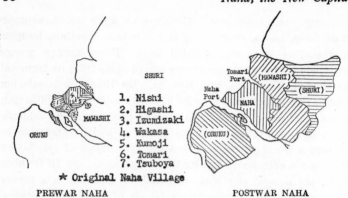

1. Nishi
2. Higashi
3. Izumizaki
4. Wakasa
5. Kumoji
6. Tomari
7. Tsuboya

★ Original Naha Village

PREWAR NAHA   POSTWAR NAHA

by Mayor Toma, brother of the present Chief Executive Jugo Toma. With an eye to expected long range advantages, Shuri and Oroku agreed to merge with Naha on September 1, 1954; and, in September 1957, Mawashi relinquished her independent status and was incorporated in the booming city. As U.S. troop installations vacated the area between Naha and Tomari ports, local construction moved in. Since 1953, the Naha picture has been a steady progress of new construction of varied design—from the small, typical, wooden residence to the storied concrete firm and factory.

This tour suggests a few of the places to visit in the capital city, (exclusive of its industries, which are covered in other tours) and some vantage points for panoramic views of this area. Roughly the tour goes into the area between Highway 1 and the main street for a stop at the Children's Museum, returns to join the stream of traffic on the road to Shuri and to travel the length of Makishi-Kokusai Street. It leaves the city by the roads on its eastern fringe.

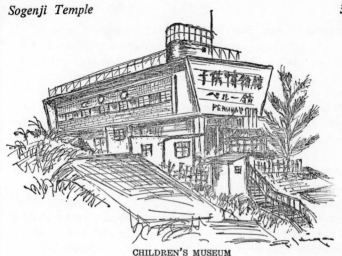

CHILDREN'S MUSEUM

Children's Museum — Located in 10-ku, Naha near the Okinawa Times. this building was built in 1952 at a cost of 2,000,000 yen. Included in the building fund was 1,300,000 yen from the Okinawan Association in Peru, South America; so the Museum is also called "Peru-Kan". It is dedicated to young people and contains display rooms of social and natural history and a projection room. Admission fees are 8¢ for adults, 6¢ for high school students, and 4¢ for children below high school age.

Sogenji Temple — The temple site is located on the road to Shuri in Tomari-cho, Naha. It was known as the "Rei-tokuzan", and was the mausoleum of the succeeding kings of Shuri from King Shun Ten down. Where once stood the old building, now stands the Ryukyuan-American

Cultural Center.   Part of the original stone wall remains.   It is very well proportioned, having the same arrangement as the famous Madan Bashi.   In the higher center portion, are 3 arched gates; on either side are lower sections, each with one gate.   These gates cut a conspicuous figure among Okinawan stone constructions, being very continental; and were praised by Dr. Chuta Ito, cultural expert from Japan, as the most beautiful constructions in the Ryukyus.   Part of the stone wall was damaged in the last war, but the Association for the Preservation of Historical Sites collected more than one million yen and sucessfully repaired it with assistance from USGAR.   The "Dismount" sign was, fortunately, saved from war damage.   In olden times, worshippers were forbidden to ride past the temple.   In order to exhibit reverence for the kings who were buried here, all were compelled to dismount 100 yards from the entrance and to walk past the shrine.

Kokusai   The northern section of the boulevard is com-
Boulevard   monly called Makishi Street and runs through
                 Naha City from Naha Police Station to the
Asato tridentate road.   Modern buildings stand along this street which is the shopping center of the city.   All sorts of shops, department stores, and office buildings line both sides of the street which, as late as 1948, was a rutted jeep track boasting a single façade, the Ernie Pyle movie theater.

One can view the city from the top of Yamagataya Department Store, which is located about midway down the street. At the north end of the street is the Ryuei Theatre, the largest building in the Asato sub-division.   The tall building on the east side of the Ryuei is the Labor Department of the

RYUKYUAN-AMERICAN CULTURAL CENTER

Government of the Ryukyus. To the right, far back on the hill, you can see the buildings of Ryukyu University. In the foreground, the roof of the Grand Orion Theater protrudes, and to the right of it you see a flight of spiral stairs on a tall building in front of the Taiho Theater; this is the Tomo-yose Department Store and the steps lead to a restaurant on the roof. The market street (Heiwa Street) begins here and runs into the old "Black Market Area", now a respectable section of small shops, restaurants, beauty parlors, and barber shops.

In front of the Yamagataya store is the Tairyu building, the Matsuzakaya building which is a Japanese cloth specialty store. South of these is the rounded roof of the Kokuei Theater. Farther south on Kokusai Boulevard are the Kishimoto buildings; at the end of the street, is the Naha Police Station, with the USCAR-GRI buildings to its left. Looking far behind the Kokuei Theater you can see buildings inside a brick wall; this is the Ryukyu Central Prison; near it is the children's park.

Facing to the west, you can view the whole picture of Naha-Tomari Ports and the rapidly building area on either side of Highway 1. To the far left are Naha Port and the Nami-no-ue Shrine area. Near at hand is the Yamashiro Watch Store with a large clock on its wall. Due west from your vantage point on Yamagataya's roof is the Children's Museum and closer in are the Okiei and Taiho Theaters. On the far right, the new Showa Bus Company building shows its large roof. On the hill beyond and above Tomari Port is the Naha-Machinato American housing area. Viewing the city in the evening from this location it is a marvelous sight with all the neon light signs blinking gaily on and off.

Ryukyu   This striking, oriental styled, two-story build-
Police   ing is one of the few structures in this area
Department   that survived World War II. It is now head-
                  quarters for all the police business of the
Ryukyu Islands, exercising control over all the police stations in the islands. Here the department chief, Mr. Nishira, and his staff work hard day and night serving the public. One of the important functions performed here is the controlling of the short wave radios which are installed in the police patrol cars. Before the war, the building was used as a gymnasium; many young men trained here in Judo and Kendo (Japanese fencing). An annual championship tournament was held with a large, enthusiastic crowd attending. The

RYUKYU POLICE DEPARTMENT

building was only slightly damaged in the war, and was used by the Americans first as a Quartermaster Officers' Club, then as an Air Force Service Club before being returned to the city of Naha. Today, the Physical Training Association is requesting that the building be returned to them for its original use as a gymnasium.

Naha Police School — Located in Miebashi-cho, Naha between the Naha Police Station and the Bus Terminal, this reinforced concrete building was built in 1953 at a cost of 6,500,000 yen. Its three stories have a total floor space of 396 tsubo (2376 sq. ft.). All the Okinawan police are trained here.

| Government of the Ryukyus Buildings | These are located in the Miebashi section of Naha City, just east of the south end of Kokusai Boulevard. Here the team known as USCAR-GRI administers the affairs of the Ryukyu Islands. |

Prior to World War II, the Ryukyu Islands were a prefecture of Japan and an integral part of the homeland. The government consisted of four Departments: General Affairs, Economics, Education, and Police Affairs; and there was a Prefectural Assembly whose acts were subject to veto by the *chiji* (governor). This *chiji* was appointed by the Prime Minister in Tokyo from party ranks; there was never a *chiji* who was a native of the islands. Moreover, island functions such as Postal Affairs, Courts, Communications, and Taxation were outside the jurisdiction of the Prefectural Government and were administered directly from Tokyo.

Initial U.S. control was administered by the Navy. On 1 July 1946, the Army assumed control with the designation "Ryukyus Command". The Commanding General was named Military Governor. Evolution of the present government of the Ryukyus under American sponsorship began in January 1946 with the creation of the Okinawan Department of Education. By April 13, departments had been established and an Okinawan governor appointed. The initial step in the direction of self-government for the Okinawan people was the 1948 election of mayors and assemblymen in the cities, towns and villages. Prewar voters in Okinawa Prefecture had elected their assemblymen and these in turn elected the mayors, so this was the first time the people elected their mayors directly.

Prior to 1952, there was no central Ryukyuan government.

THE EXECUTIVE BUILDING

The islands were divided into 4 *guntos* (groups): Amami O-Shima, Chinawa, Miyako, and Yaeyama. When American Military Government was redesigned United States Civil Administration of the Ryukyuan Islands on 5 December 1950, new objectives for the Ryukyus were set forth. Among them were plans for the establishment of a central government for all the islands. This step had been recommended by the Okinawa Mayors' Association and the Gunto Governors' Conference. On 18 December 1951, an Election Law was published by the Civil Administrator establishing 8 electoral districts for the entire Ryukyus from which 31 legislators were to be chosen. The elections were held on 3 March 1952. On 1 April 1952 the government of the Ryukyu Islands passed to this elected body and the Chief Executive and Deputy Chief who were appointed by the U.S. High Commissioner.

The   In April 1953, the government moved into the
Executive   new Executive Building shown here. Designed
Building   by Japanese architects and built by the Okinawan firm of Kokuba Gumi, it has a total floor
space of 1541 *tsubo* and was completed in 1½ years at a cost of
96,000,000 yen—an even $800,000. It is a four story, reinforced
concrete building and boasted the first passenger elevator on
Okinawa. In addition to suites for the Civil Administrator,
the Chief Executive, and the Directors of the various departments, it contains a restaurant and barber shop. Here the
team known as USCAR-GRI administers the Ryukyu Islands.

The   In accordance with the principle of separation
Legislative   of the three branches of government, the Ryu-
Building   kyuan Legislature made its start with the 1952
election. In June 1953, the construction of the
building to house it was started. A year later, in June 1954,
it was completed at a cost of 24,600,000 yen. It has a total
floor space of 692 *tsubo,* and is equipped with various modern
facilities, containing individual rooms for the members, an
assembly hall, committee rooms, and library.

The   Constructed to house the third branch of govern-
Judicial   ment, this is a T-shaped building, south of the
Building   Executive Building with a total floor space of
851 *tsubo*. The construction was started on 9
May, 1955 by the Kokuba Gumi construction company and
completed on 31 March, 1956. The total cost was 19,610,000
yen. The building contains the Ryukyu Court of Appeals,
the Central Court of Assize, the Shimajiri Court of Assize

(southern area), the Naha Magistrate Court, and the Ryukyu Domestic Relations Court.

Children's   The Children's Park (Yu En Chi). On the hill
Park   east of Naha High School and known as "Gu-
              suku Dake", this was a miniature Coney Island
opened in 1951 with private capital. There was a ferris wheel,
a miniature railroad, a mechanical boat ride, a small zoo,
theater, and refreshment stands. The equipment has deteriorated, and today it is principally a spot where the city people
come to enjoy a cool evening or to watch the pageants and
tournaments staged at Naha High School field on Sunday
afternoons. There is a good view from here of the Naha-Shuri
area and many use this spot for taking pictures.

Naha   Located in Sobe-ku, Naha, east of the Children's
Central   Park, the prison was built in 1926 and has the
Prison   customary high brick wall with spaced watch
              towers. It has recently been enlarged and modi-
fied. In 1926, the prison population was given as 266 (254
male and 12 female). Statistics for 1955, give a total of 845
prisoners, 828 male and 17 female.

Chief   The "Shuseki Ko-sha" stands in the Yogi-ku
Executive's   section of Mawashi. The site used to be a
Residence   small forest. The building was completed in
              1955 and occupied by the first Chief Executive
of the Government of the Ryukyus, Mr. Shuhei Higa. The
present occupant is Mr. Jugo Toma, who succeeded Mr. Higa.
The residence is a two-story concrete building with eastern

and western style rooms. It is on a hill within a landscaped
area surrounded by a fence. A police guard is posted at the
entrance gate 24 hours a day. Guided tours are conducted
through the residence and may be pre-arranged through the
Army Service Clubs.

Southern Okinawa: Naha & Tomari Port Areas

Okinawa's two principal ports are on the East China Sea. In early history, Tomari was the base for foreign trade. But the Chokotei dyke, constructed in the early fifteenth century by King Sho Kimpuku, enlarged the facilities of Naha and the bulk of the trade shifted there. It was at Naha Port that Commodore Perry landed. At present the larger commercial ships come into Naha Port which is shared with the American military transportation service; but the bustle of commercial and passenger traffic has shifted to Tomari. A number of interesting places developed around the two ports and the capital city of Naha.

Ono Yama Park

Located to the east of Naha harbor, this site used to be an island, but the two original bridges have been replaced by land fills. This small islet was the only park in the prewar city of Naha. It was opened in commemoration of the marriage of the Emperor Taisho, and contained the marriage monument, the Russo-Japanese War Memorial, the Yomochi and Gokoku Shrines, and a statue to Narahara (a governor of Okinawa). There was a large playground on the northern side, the flying waterfall of Utenda on the south, and, on the east, a small island of Gahnah wood floated in the water. A beautiful view of the entire city of Naha could be seen when one stood in the park. The last war killed all the big trees, destroyed the

1. Onoyama Park.
2. Nami-no-Ue.
3. Naha Cent. Post Office.
4. Wakamatsu Street.
5. Tomari.
6. International Cemetery.
7. Ryukyu Weather Bureau.
8. Naha Reservoir.

monuments and statues, and reduced the two shrines to ashes. Today, the Gokoku and Yomochi shrines have been rebuilt. "Yomochi" means "save the world"; this shrine is dedicated to the following three great men.

Noguni Sokan At one time, Okinawa was so short of foodstuffs that the people were faced with starvation. To alleviate the famine, the governor had ordered that all persons over 60 years old should be abandoned. Noguni Sokan brought to Okinawa from China sweet potato seedlings which he planted in Chatan village (Sukiran-Kue area). From here they spread all over the island. The new planting of sweet potatoes saved many lives. The sweet potato became Okinawa's main crop, accounting for 50% of the planted acreage.

Gima Shinjo About 330 years ago Gima Shinjo brought sugar manufacturing techniques from China and circulated them about the island. He also organized the agricultural industry and started the textile industry.

Saion Born in Naha in 1682 Saion studied at a college in China and returned to Okinawa in 1700. He then became the tutor of Prince Shokei. When Shokei became king at the age of 14, he appointed Saion as one of his ministers. In this capacity he reorganized the administration, its agriculture and industry. He was a great statesman, and lived to the venerable age of 80.

The memorial *torii* at the entrance to Ono Yama Park withstood the bombings of World War II. It was so sacred to Okinawan culture that, when the land on which it stood was needed for the present highway, it was carefully moved by U.S. engineers to the site just off the highway where it now stands.

Meiji Bashi This is the bridge which spans the Kokuba river as it enters Naha harbor. The original bridge was totally destroyed in the Battle of Okinawa. The present one was erected in 1953, under the supervision of the Okinawa Engineer District of the U.S. Far East Command, by the Sugawara Construction Company and fabricated by the Harima Ship Building Works—both Japanese firms.

Nami-no-ue This name which means "over the waves" is the name of the cliff just north of Naha Port in the Wakasa-machi section of Naha City. It is recommended for its beautiful views. Facing the East China Sea you see the Kerama Islands on the western horizon; to the east you overlook the whole of Naha City with the hills of Shuri in the distance. There is a shrine, temple, skating rink, monuments, a swimming pool, and many boats for rent. The swimming pool is built into the sea and was originally part of a commercial hotel which stood below the cliff prior to World War II. The war reduced the entire area to rubble; only the three *torii* and a few stone lanterns were left standing.

Nami-no-ue Gu This shrine stands on top of the coral cliff; it was the only Japanese government supported shrine on Okinawa. In the main building the god Izanami-no-Mikoto was enshrined. To the left was the god, Hayatamao-no-Mikoto, and to the right Kotowakeo-no-Mikoto. On May 17th every year a great festival was held for them.

YOMOCHI SHRINE

It is not clear when the shrine was opened, but reputedly the gods were invited from Kuma-no-Gongen (a shrine in Japan) as protectors of the state lands. It was ranked as a government shrine, Class C (lowest) in 1890. Rehabilitation was begun in 1953 and has been steadily carried on with donations from Hawaii. The first of the three *torii* was razed in 1955 to make way for the road connecting Naha and Tomari ports. The stone lanterns along the entrance avenue are memorials given by individuals and groups; the smaller ones cost $100. The annual Juri Uma festival, in which the dancers from the various teahouses participate, is held at this shrine, starting from the "Under the Pine Tree Teahouse" to which Americans

NAMI-NO-UE GU

gave the name "Teahouse of the August Moon" which is just south of the steps to the shrine.

Gokoku-   Also known as Nami-no-ue-tera, this was the
Ji   first-ranking temple of the Shingon sect. In
           olden times the kings prayed here. There is some doubt as to when it was founded; but the story is told that 560 years ago a Japanese monk, Raiju, lived in this temple. It is also said that, in the reign of King Sho-Shin, a monk named Nisshu endeavored to teach the Buddhist beliefs here in this temple. Everything was destroyed by fire in the last war except a preaching stone of the monk, Nisshu. Only the Bettleheim Memorial and the tombstone of the "Formosa

GOKOKU-JI

Sufferers" remained. The latter were 54 men who were drowned in 1869 when caught in a typhoon which drifted their ship to Formosa. The shrine, with its Japanese bridge and garden, has been restored through the efforts of a postwar caretaker who solicited adherents of this faith in Hawaii and others. There are a number of interesting monuments in this area.

The Bettelheim Memorial — Following is a translation of the writing on this memorial which stands near Gokokuji: "Dr. Bettelheim was sent to Okinawa as a missionary from the Naval Mission Group of Great Britain. He lived in Naha with his family between

1846 and 1854. At that time the Ryukyuan government forbade Christian preaching, so he gave medical treatment to the people and introduced vaccination techniques to the Okinawans. He also translated the Bible to the Okinawan language."

Kozakura-   On May 5, 1954 Mr. Katsura Kawai, President
no-To   of the Suzushiro Children's Association in
               Aichi Prefecture of Japan, came to Okinawa
with his advisor, Mr. Asakichi Matsura to build this memorial to the souls of 5,000 Okinawan school children who died in World War II. The children were on a ship which was transporting them to sanctuary in Japan during the heavy fighting on Okinawa. The ship was attacked and destroyed at sea. The monument is inscribed with a poem of condolence:

"Oh, they have passed away like flowers
Falling on the blue sea! Poor short lives!
Though springs come back again
I see those faces who do not come back again!"

Wako   The Wako Jizo Son image of Buddha stands on
Buddha   top of Nami-no-ue hill. It is dedicated to the
Image   spirits who died in World War II to pray that they
              attain Buddhahood, and also for peace in this world, and happiness for human beings. It was presented by a group of believers of the Shiten-o Temple in Japan in May 1952. This is one of three Wako Jizo Son statues on Okinawa; the others are at the Unknown Soldier Monument, near the Cave of the Virigins, and at Urasoe. (*Wa* means friendship and peace; *ko* means light, hope, happiness.)

A fourth monument at Nami-no-ue is the Policemen's

KOZAKURA-NO-TO

Monument erected in November 1954 by Police Director
Kenshin Nakamura and his staff as a memorial to those who
lost their lives in the line of duty as public protectors.

Public   The Naha Central Post Office Building is
Services   located in Matsuyama-cho, Naha, just north
Department   of the entrance to the Nami-no-ue area. It
                was built in December 1952 at a cost of
¥27,430,000.   It is a U-shaped building of two stories with
a total floor space of 371 *tsubo*. Located on the first floor
are the Naha Central Post Office, the Naha Central Telegraph
Office, and the Ryukyus International Telecommunications
Service (RITS). On the second floor are the Public Service
Department and the Naha Central Telephone Exchange.

Wakamatsu   In 1956 a long, straight street of modern
Commercial   buildings was constructed in what was the
Street   commercial area of prewar Naha, Matsuyama-
                   cho. This area lies between Naha and Tomari
Ports, and is an ideal site for future commercial enterprises.
The main thoroughfare is called Wakamatsu (young pine
tree) Commercial Street. The more than 60 two-to four-story
concrete buildings are all occupied by wholesale merchants;
the upper floors of some are modern living apartments. The
Benbo Lacquer Factory and the Ryukyu Oil Company are in
this neighborhood.

In the area between Wakamatsu Street and the East China
Sea, there is a new, large, municipal low-cost housing development consisting of individual homes, duplex units, and 4-story
apartment buildings. Rents are as low as $10 per month for
a small apartment in this city-sponsored project.

The entire Wakamatsu area was opened in November 1956
with a big open-air ceremony; new buildings and enterprises
are increasing day by day.

Tomari   Situated at the mouth of the Asato River. This
Harbor   was the principal harbor in the Ryukyus before
                Naha Port was constructed. The thriving port
town of Tomari was on the north shore of the harbor. About
500 years ago, King Sho-Toku came back to this harbor tri-
umphantly after conquering the northern offshore island of
Kikai Jima and appointed the lord of Tomari to administer
his northern conquests. A famous bridge, Tomari Takahashi,
connected Tomari with the south shore town of Katabaru.
It is said that this was a foreign town in old times, like International Settlements in the United States, where people from

different countries of Europe and Asia lived. The stone bridge was cut in half in the last war and a steel bridge built by American engineers has replaced it. Following the war, most of the Tomari area was occupied by U.S. military installations and one of the military cemeteries was located here. At this time, Tomari Port was just an anchorage for small fishing boats.

But as soon as the U.S. installations moved out, commercial and residential building began. Tomari is once again a thriving port with a new Port Office building which was completed in 1958. Passenger and cargo vessels enter and leave here almost every day in the week, plying a lucrative trade between Okinawa, the other Ryukyuan Islands, and Japan.

International   Located on the north shore of Tomari harbor
Cemetery   near the Okinawa Cement Company factory,
                the cemetery is a small, wooded oasis in this
busy commercial area. It was set aside as a burial ground for foreigners in the nineteenth century when a number of western countries were sending trade missions to Okinawa. Among the earliest interments were a French priest and an English seaman. The latter was from H.M.S. "Alceste" which visited Naha in 1816. A number of the members of Admiral Perry's expedition are also buried here. For nearly a century after Perry, no new graves were added, but a row of small recent graves are those of American infants who died on Okinawa during the American occupation. The following are old and readable tombs in the cemetery:

J. J. Doss Bornibib   —1843 Eli Crose, USN   —1854
Jesse L. Carter, USN   —1854 John Williams, USN   —1854

John Barnes, USN	—1853	John Miller, USN	—1854
W.M. Hares, British		William Board,	
Navy	—1816	USN	—1854
Hugh Ellis, USN	—1853	H. E. Amoore	—1908

Damaged in World War II, the cemetery was restored in June 1955 by the city of Naha with the assistance of USCAR.

Tomari   Tomari was built in 1933 in Uenoya, and was
Reservoir   the largest water reservoir on Okinawa.   It was
              damaged in the last war and was repaired by the
U.S. forces and used to supply water to U.S. troop installations
in the Naha area, but has now been returned to Naha city.
The reservoir has a capacity of 3,000,000 gallons; but the
daily consumption of Naha city is 3,500,000 gallons and
finding an additional water source is one of the city's big
problems.

Ryukyu   Standing on a hill above Ameku Village near
Weather   Tomari Port, the weather bureau occupies a total
Bureau   ground space of 4,126 *tsubo*.   Major buildings
              at the installation are: the Main Building, the
Wind Measuring Building, the Earthquake Measuring Building, the Wireless Telegraphy Building, and a new radar tower
20 meters high.   The station was built in 1953 by the Government of the Ryukyus at a cost of 3,000,000 yen.   A total of 66
scientists and assistants work here; and a staff of 82 in the
Ishigaki branch on Yaeyama Island and the Miyako branch
on Miyako Island.   They track the weather, reporting every
hour, protecting ships and people from weather calamity,
especially typhoons.   The radar equipment, costing 6,920,000
yen was installed in August 1958 by three engineers from

Japan. The radar has the power of 300 kilowatts, 5,300 megacycles; it is able to catch the exact location of a typhoon 186 miles away. This is a great help for the Ryukyus, Japan, and Formosa.

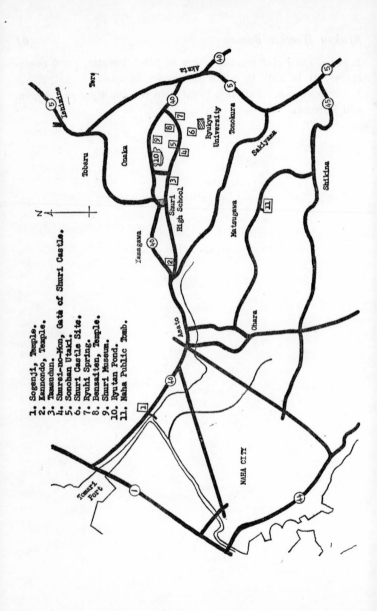

1. Sogenji, Temple.
2. Kannondo, Temple.
3. Tamaudun.
4. Shurei-no-Mon, Gate of Shuri Castle.
5. Sonohan Utaki.
6. Shuri Castle Site.
7. Ryuhi Spring.
8. Bensaiten, Temple.
9. Shuri Museum.
10. Ryutan Pond.
11. Naha Public Tomb.

Shuri, the Old Capital

Shuri was the center of politics, education, religion, and the arts and worthy of its function as the capital for over 1000 years. There were 23 examples of buildings and works of art within the city which were designated as National Treasures. The old King's Castle, the residence of Marquis Sho, Shurei-no-Mon, Ryutan Pond, Tama-Undun Mausoleum, and Yomochi Bashi is a partial list. All of these precious treasures were lost in the last war. The Shuri Museum now preserves the remains of some, which have been excavated from the ashes of war, and the facsimiles of others.

When the Ryukyus became a prefecture of Japan in 1849, Naha was made the capital. But Shuri remained the elite and cultural center to the extent that many well-to-do Okinawans living abroad, even in North and South America, sent their children back to Shuri to school. Since 1950 Shuri has been gradually returning to its former cultural position and, among the public places of interest, there are many new, elegant residences of families in the top income bracket.

Shuri Museum With the Perry Memorial Annex, the museum contains 12,409 exhibits—relics of ancient Shuri Castle as well as examples of Ryukyuan art and handicrafts. There are models of the castle and of Shurei-no-Mon, the famous second gate to the castle grounds. This beautiful gate, whose name means "land of courtesy" was the subject of many paintings. Here also are the large

Enkaku-ji Temple bell and the smaller Shuri Castle bell. The knobs on the bells measure resonance of sound. The long inscription on the castle bell begins, "In the southern seas lie the islands of the Ryukyu kingdom, known widely for their scenic beauty . . ." and goes on to describe the importance of a bell in the life of the community.

Along the walls of the museum are examples of native fabrics, including early prints of the famous *bingata* dye process, and ancient scrolls. In the cases are articles of mother-of-pearl, gold, and lacquer. Especially interesting are the old lacquer boxes for carrying official documents, the *ofu* (picnic box), and the jewelry worn by the Shuri kings on the day of their ascension to the throne, and the coins of the old realm.

At the entrance to the museum are two *shi-shi* (dogs), carved out of stone, which once stood at the head of the tomb of the kings. In the courtyard is a reconstruction of the bridge that once spanned the Hojo Ike ("Set-Free-and-Let-Live Pond") on the castle grounds. According to ancient custom, when fish, turtles, or other marine life were released into this pond by relatives of a deceased person the latter was aided in the next world by the generosity of this act.

Ryutan   This pond is situated in front of the former resi-
Pond   dence of Marquis Sho of the first dynasty. Ex-
           cavated about 520 years ago, it is more than 2 miles in circumference and has an area of about 16,000 square feet. It is said that in olden times *haryu-sen* (boat races) were held on this pond on the festive day of September 9 to accord the visiting Chinese mission warm hospitality. The Yomochi Bashi (bridge) was moved to this pond from the

SONOHAN UTAKI STONE GATE

temple known as Jion-ji in 1661 in the reign of Sho Shitsu; it was ornamented with a series of fish and shell engravings peculiar to the southern area. Although these designs were a valuable asset to the study of the arts of the ancient Ryukyus, they were destroyed in the last war.

Bensaiten Next to Ryutan Pond beside a University of the
Pond Ryukyus dormitory lies Bensaiten Pond. Here, in ancient times there stood a temple, Bensaiten-do, in which were enshrined the Holy Buddhist Scriptures presented to the Ryukyus by the king of Korea. In 1609, during the battle with Satsuma of Kagoshima, Japan, the temple and the scriptures were destroyed. In 1621, during

the reign of King Sho-Ho, the temple was rebuilt. In it was enshrined the Bensaiten Buddha from Enkaku-Ji temple. Both the temple and Buddha were destroyed in World War II; today there remains only a part of the bridge.

Sonohan Utaki Stone Gate
Once this gate marked the entrance to a sacred grove of trees (*utaki* means holy ground) in which in ancient times the king prayed for a safe return whenever he made a tour. Tradition says that, if there was an impending misfortune in the king's tour outside the castle, the god would appear before him and notify him of the trouble. The gate itself was built by King Shoshin in the 16th century and is a valuable example of the uniqueness of the Ryukyuan architecture of that time with its harmonious beauty of semi-Chinese style in the gable roof and rafters. In the neighborhood stood the oldest stone monument in the Ryukyus depicting the trees and blossoms of Ankokuzan hill and erected in the reign of King Sho-Hashi. The gate was designated as a national treasure by the Japanese government. Almost completely destroyed during the Battle of Okinawa, the gate was restored by the Cultural Property Protection Commission in 1956.

Ryuhi Spring
This spring is on the Shuri Castle site near the entrance to the Shikiya Library of the University. It was used for the water supply of Shuri Castle. The spring ran out from the mouth of a dragon shaped stone which was brought to Okinawa in 1517 from China (some say on the bottom of a ship whose crew had illegally procured it). The dragon became a popular symbol for stone sculpture on Okinawa. The carved stone was destroyed in the war,

SHURI CASTLE SITE

but the spring water still runs freely through a wire screen which protects its source.

Shuri Castle Site
The site now occupied by the University of the Ryukyus was Shuri Castle, home and fortress of the kings of the Ryukyus. The original castle, built in 1188 under the Shunten Dynasty, was enlarged in 1350 by the Satto Dynasty, and again in 1422 by the first Sho king. But it was the famous Sho-Shin, the first ruler during what is called Okinawa's "Golden Age" (1477 to 1609), who enlarged and remodelled the castle and beautified the surroundings, creating the Shuri Castle which survives in art and tradition.

It was an immense castle, 225 *ken* (1350 ft.) in the east-west directions, 150 *ken* (900 ft.) in the north-south directions and

19,000 *tsubo* (54,000 sq. ft.) in area. The main hall was the largest building in the Ryukyus, towering into the clouds, and was called the *Momburasoe* (Ruler's Palace). It was also popularly called the "Chinese Gable" because of its style. Around the main hall were stone railings, and at the foot of the stone stairs in front of the entrance there were two stone pillars cut in the shape of curious dragons. Important buildings beside the main hall were the north and south halls. The north hall was also called "Nishinu Udun" and was built in pure Chinese style to receive the Chinese Mission. The south hall was called "Haenu Udun" and was built in pure Japanese style to receive the Satsuma Mission from Kagoshima. In those days, the Ryukyuan king was an important intermediary in Japan-China affairs. The castle was surrounded by deep moats and massive walls within which were beautiful gardens. From its high hill, it commanded a magnificent view of rugged mountains, low plains, and the East China Sea. It was a fit palace for a proud king.

When the last King, Sho-Tai was deposed by the Japanese in 1879, the castle became a National Museum. By 1922, the main hall had so deteriorated that razing it was considered. However, through the efforts of a Dr. Ito, means were found to restore and preserve it as a shrine dedicated to the Shuntens and Shos who built it. During the last war, the castle served as a Japanese Army Headquarters and its gardens became a drill ground. The castle was destroyed to the last leaf of grass during the long hard battle for Shuri in World War II.

The castle site was selected as a fitting location for the University of the Ryukyus which was opened in November, 1950; the Ryukyus Broadcasting Station was also located here in February, 1953. And on 30, March, 1958, in a colorful *Gohi*

KANNON TEMPLE

Bibishit—"Ceremony for the Hauling of Honorable Trees"—
the reconstruction of Shurei-no-Mon was begun. The gate
pillars (22-foot oak logs, weighing 1500 lbs. each, some of them
700-800 years old) were cut in Kunigami, northern Okinawa,
transported to Shuri by trucks, and pulled 450 feet to the
construction site by Shuri School students singing the "Timber
Carriers' Song". The logs were tied to platforms with red
and white ropes; a table in front of the platforms was laid
with the traditional offerings of fish, fruit, and wine. Here
the Ryukyuan dignitaries placed a token branch beseeching
blessings on the project. The logs, themselves, were blessed
by two Shinto priests in a majestic and colorful ritual. The
logs were placed at the entrance to Shuri Museum on the spot
where the original gate stood. The rebuilding of Shurei-no-

Mon is a project co-sponsored by the Society for the Complete
Restoration of Shuri Gate and the Cultural Assets Committee.
The cost of 2.5 million yen was borne by the Ryukyuan-
American Relations Committee, GRI, and public contributions.

Tama-   At Kanagusuku, Shuri, stands the tomb of
Udun   the successive generations of the Sho house,
Mausoleum   and was built in 1501 by King Sho-Shin
               to re-inter the ashes of his father, King
Sho-En. In the cemetery there were three imposing old Ryukyuan style tombs. It is said that the one in the center was
where the coffin of the dead rested until the washing of the
bones; after the washing ceremony, the bones of the kings
were transferred to the tomb on the left, those of the queens
to the one on the right. Tama Udun was destroyed in World
War II; but the magnificence and dexterity of its construction
are still remembered.

City   This stands in the Shikina village near Shuri, on the
Public   old site of Shikina-En. It became necessary to
Burial   move the family tombs in Naha City because of
Vault   the city reconstruction plan and the U.S. military
               plan. Since there was no extra land on which to
build individual tombs for such a large population, the city
decided to build a public burial vault. It is a cross-shaped
building. Both sides command wonderful views of the whole
of Naha City and of Shuri.

Kannon-   This has long been a beloved shrine for Okina-
do   wans. In 1616, when the royal prince, Sho-Ho,
Temple   was held hostage by the Satsumas in Kagoshima,

Japan, his father, Sho-Kyu made supplication to the Buddhist deity for the safe return of his son. His prayer was answered; Sho-Ho returned to Okinawa in the next year. The king was so happy that he erected this temple to the god who had granted his favor. Thereafter the whole Ryukyuan population worshipped it as a shrine to the god of navigation. The shrine was popularized in a song by Choki Yakabi entitled *Nobori-Kuduchi*; the Okinawan dance to this tune dramatizes Kannon's protection of travellers. The main building and its additions were entirely destroyed in the last war, but a priest begged donations from the whole of the Ryukyus for its restoration. The new temple was completed on June 29, 1952 and continues to be a favorite shrine, especially for those who are embarking on journeys or whose family members are travelling away from home.

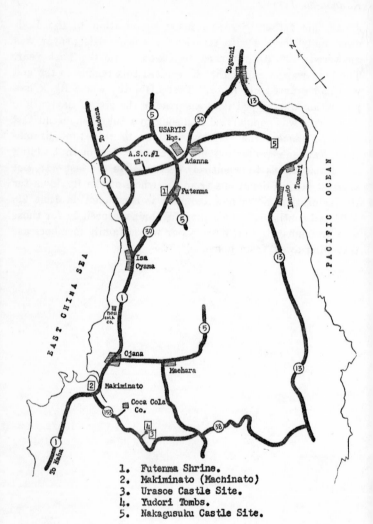

1. Futenma Shrine.
2. Makiminato (Machinato)
3. Urasoe Castle Site.
4. Yudori Tombs.
5. Nakagusuku Castle Site.

Central Okinawa: Futenma and Nakagusuku Areas

Futenma Shrine Entering the *torii* (a shrine gate), you will see a sanctuary and a cave in which the goddess is enshrined. It is a stalactite grotto and inside numerous stalactites hang down, presenting a remarkable sight. In the center of Futenma, it is one of the eight famous shrines on Okinawa. It has been worshipped and visited by many people, as it is said that it works miracles. In the last war, the cave was used for a natural dugout, which saved many noncombatants' lives. The shrine was restored in June 1953, with a contribution from the Hawaii Isshin-Club of $1,000 and with funds collected from Ryukyuan adherents.

A legend says that a samurai forgot his sword in Futenma Shrine and remembered it on the ship on his way to Kagoshima, Japan. He prayed to the god of Futenma Shrine asking: "Please keep my sword until I come back to Okinawa." So whenever anyone came close to the sword it was transformed into a snake or a stake. When he came back to Okinawa he visited the Futenma Shrine because of the sword, and was surprised to find that it was safe in the original place at the Futenma Shrine. After this, many people respected this shrine as the abode of protecting life and property.

Makiminato (Machinato) The Machinato river flows on the borderline between Urasoe-son and Ginowan-son. The place is of interest as it was used for the port of trades in the olden times when Urasoe was the capital of Ryukyus and was called "Machiminato". It is said that Minamoto Tametomo set sail from this port, while his wife and children waited for him here, and thus it came to be called *Machi* (wait), *minato* (port). It is also said that Satto bartered gold here through Japanese merchants, for iron made there with agricultural tools distributed among farmers. He was nominated for king, and later enthroned. It is inferred from the above that this place was then used for the port of trades. In later years, when Chinese vessels were anchoring at Naha Port, the vessels of the Satsuma clan took refuge in this port to hide themselves. This place was also one of the hard fought fields in the last war, and the port, including piers and other constructions, were totally destroyed. But, after the war, U.S. Forces constructed Highway No. 1 and established here a power plant.

Urasoe   Here stood an impregnable castle with its surround-
Castle   ing coral reef cliff, north of Maeda, Urasoe-son.
Site   Urasoe etymologically means "to govern all over
             the country". As a number of the kings, such as
Shunten, Eiso and Satto were all born at Urasoe, it is concluded that it actually ruled over the Ryukyuan Islands. Moreover, from the fact that old tiles were unearthed from the Urasoe Castle site, and Machinato was the port of trades in olden times, it is judged that the Urasoe Castle had once been the site of a thriving capital town. The site was a hard fought field in the last war, and now a stone image of Wako-Jizo stands there. "Wako-Jizo" means "Peace-Light". There are several such monuments newly erected on Okinawa. In the

FUTENMA SHRINE

cave below the statue are bones of war dead from this area.

Yudori   Just east of the old castle site in Urasoe are the
Tombs   Yudori tombs. One of those tombs was built about
              650 years ago by King Eiso during his lifetime.
He called it "Mountain of Paradise". It was renamed "Yudori" at his death. The word *yudori* means "the evening
breeze". The evening breeze is soft and gentle compared
to the harsh, hot winds of the day so, in naming the tomb
"Yudori", Eiso was indicating the loss of vigor which comes
to man in his old age. About 362 years later, Sho-nei, 7th
king of the 2nd Sho dynasty (1590-1622), having lost the battle

YUDORI TOMBS

of Keicho, ordered his retainer to build his tomb to the left of
Eiso. He thus acknowledged his shame at having lost power
by choosing to be buried at Yudori. Both tombs were destroyed by the last war, but investigators studying Okinawan
culture discovered on the site a stone coffin and a sculpture that
were fine examples of Okinawan arts of olden times. To
preserve these for all people interested in Okinawan culture,
the tombs were restored.

The Castle Site of Nakagusuku	The building of this castle dates back to 1454 when ten thousand Okinawans labored for ten years to build a castle for their lord Gosamaru to help protect the kingdom of Shuri. Back- breaking labor went into the building of this

NAKAGUSUKU CASTLE SITE

now legendary castle whose every stone had to be carried to the summit of the cliff and fitted by hand.

The story of Nakagusuku is one of the most dramatic episodes of Okinawan history. Moriharu Gosamaru, the lord of Zakimi Castle at Yomitan, whose daughter was King Sho-taiku's wife, was one of the king's most faithful retainers. To strengthen his Shuri defenses, Sho-taiku gave Gosamaru the lands around Nakagusuku and requested him to build a castle on the high hill there. Gosamaru realized the strategic value of this site which is 12 kilometers east of Shuri and hastened to complete the fortress. From within its walls, a look-out could cover all approaches to the castle. When the castle was finished, Gosamaru set about training his men to maintain it as an outer defense for the king's castle at Shuri.

Meantime, Amawari, lord of Katsuren Castle (near White Beach) fostered an ambition to attack Shuri, but realized that the defenses of Nakagusuku made this impossible. He then resorted to treachery. Travelling by boat to Yonabaru, he made his way to Shuri Castle and told the king that Gosamaru had turned traitor and was training his soldiers to attack Shuri. The king refused, at first, to believe this, but Amawari persuaded him that he was the one to be trusted because he had taken great risk to bring the king word of his danger. He prevailed upon Sho-taiku to send a spy to Nakagusuku; the spy returned to report that Gosamaru was indeed training his soldiers. Without further investigation, the king sent Amawari in charge of a dawn attack on Nakagusuku. Although forewarned of Amawari's treachery, the loyal Gosamaru refused to defend himself against an army carrying the king's standard.

Instead, there on the steps leading to the stone altar built in honor of the king's Gods, Gosamaru and all his warriors committed hara-kiri on the moonlight night of August 15, 1460 (in lunar calendar). The third son of Gosamaru was saved by his nurse. She fled from the castle with the child in her arms and Amawari's soldiers in pursuit. At one spot on the mountain side, the rocks parted behind her making a deep ravine which the soldiers could not cross.

According to the legend, Gosamaru placed a message for the king in his mouth so that when Amawari took his head to the king, the intrigue was discovered. But history reveals that Amawari's wife, daughter of the king, fled to Shuri and herself betrayed the treachery of her husband. A force was dispatched against the traitor, his army scattered, and Amawari executed. Gosamaru's tomb on a hillside near the castle

TURTLE-BACK TOMB

is believed to be the first of the "turtle-back" tombs, a combination of the Okinawan cave-type tomb and the mound-type grave used by the Chinese families of the Kume Village settlement in Naha. Other families, honoring Gosamaru, copied his tomb. In 1871 the Japanese erected a monument within the castle walls dedicated to soldiers who had died for their emperor, and subsequently Japanese propaganda glorified Gosamaru as a brave, loyal patriot, adding impetus to the movement.

Thus the turtle-back tomb which dots Okinawan hillsides is a comparatively modern fad, in vogue since 1871, and dating back at the very most to Gosamaru's death in 1460. Today, one may see the remnants of baths and various

foundations which were destroyed shortly after its completion
and which have never been rebuilt.

The XXXIV Corps, commanded by Major General Hodge,
had its command post located in the ruins of the castle from
10 April to 15 October 1945.

The castle has recently been landscaped and made into
Nakagusuku Castle National Park.

Central Okinawa: Awase and Katsuren Peninsula

Awase Bezuru Shrine.   Before you go into the Awase Beach, you will see a shrine gate on your right. This shrine is not Shinto, nor is it a temple; it is a village altar to a god who protects against evil spirits or diseases.

You will notice the three stones on the shelf in the shrine. Those three stones were washed on to the shore of Awase with the sea grasses many hundreds of years ago. A woman called Takaesu went to the shore and picked up those grasses for manure on her farm; then those three stones followed her like something alive. She wondered if they had come from heaven to protect the people of Awase; so she asked the village officers to make a shrine for them.   In shape the stones somewhat resemble the legs of a horse.

Awase Beach   When you get to Awase beach located about 1500 meters east of Takahara village, you can hear the noise of boat engines and see people enjoying themselves in the boats on a hot summer afternoon.   They are members of the Okinawan Yacht Club.

The membership consists of about 120 American personnel who are employed on Okinawa.   It is a nice view in front of the beach because the Katsuren peninsula stretches to Awase and makes a cove to the beach.

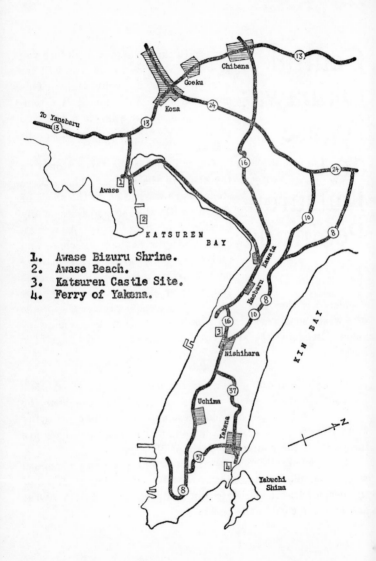

1. Awase Bizuru Shrine.
2. Awase Beach.
3. Katsuren Castle Site.
4. Ferry of Yakena.

Katsuren
Castle
Site

On the high hill in between the villages of Haebaru and Nishihara about 19 miles east of Sukiran is the site of a castle of legendary fame.

About 500 years ago, the master of the castle, Mochizuki-anji, was killed by Amawari, one of his retainers.

The castle was destroyed in 1903 for the purpose of constructing the breakwater along the coast line to Awase. Part of this breakwater is actually the old stone wall of Katsuren Castle.

Amawari-kana (who became lord of Katsuren Castle and destroyed Nakagusuku Castle) was born in the farming village of Yara just east of Kadena Circle. He was so weak in his childhood that he could not help his parents in the farming field even at the age of 14. So one day his parents took him into the forest which was at the foot of Katsuren Castle and left him there, a distance of about 15 miles from his village.

Amawari realized that his parents had abandoned him because of his weakness. He lay down to rest a while in the forest and figure out what he could do. Then he saw a spider spinning his web; when it was completed, the spider hid himself in the branches and waited for something to enter his trap. So Amawari-kana got an idea from it and he decided to make himself a fishing net. At that time there were no fishing nets on Okinawa; the fishermen in Katsuren caught fish with the bamboo baskets. The catch was so small that it was only enough to supply the samurai of the castle; the poor fishermen of Katsuren could never eat any fish. The people of Katsuren were always complaining about this. But when Amawari made his net, he caught many fish very easily.

He gave all his fish to the village fishermen and farmers; and the people of Katsuren stopped complaining about fish.

Mochizuki-anji, master of Katsuren Castle, wondered that the people of Katsuren ate fish; so he sent a man to the village to investigate. The man came back to the castle and reported to him "a farmer's son who came from Yara made a fishing net and catches fish and gives it to villagers".

Mochizuki-anji realized that the farmer's son was smart; so he appointed him to his staff in the castle. Amawari grew in strength and advanced in position at Katsuren. But Amawari kept in touch with people at Katsuren among whom he was very popular. One day he went to the village to see how they were getting along with the fishing nets. A man came up to him and told him "Mr. Amawari we have an obligation to you more than the deepest ocean or highest mountain, so we would like to help you whenever you wish". Amawari was pleased that the village people were so much devoted to him, and decided he might use them to advance himself.

He told the man "on the night of the dark moon gather all people in the village and bring them to the castle gate; also bring seven boxes of swords in a suitcase and make a torchlight procession to the castle gate. I will send someone to open the gate for you." The man promised to do it. That night Amawari asked Mochizuki-anji to go to the watchtower. When Mochizuki-anji saw the torchlights he asked Amawari, "What's going on over there?" Amawari answered, "Tonight I organized a special party because all the village people wanted to express their appreciation to you. So please let them into the castle that they may have a chance to see you and entertain you." Mochizuki-anji allowed the people to come in the castle and he said, "Tonight we drink hard and enjoy the dance." The people of Katsuren were very happy for this was their first time in the castle.

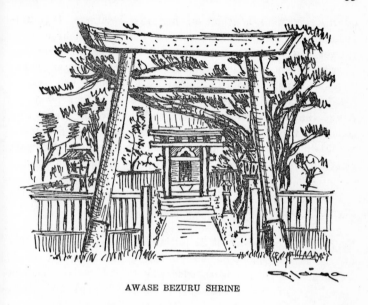

AWASE BEZURU SHRINE

Mochizuki-anji was very happy because they entertained him so well, and he emptied many bottles. Then Amawari decided to take action. He ordered the village men to get the swords and kill whoever came against them; and he opened a box, got a sword, and killed Mochizuki-anji! So he became the master of Katsuren Castle. Then he gave some money to the people of Katsuren and re-celebrated for their future.

The king of Shuri heard the story of Amawari's coup, and he ordered him to become his retainer. He was allowed to govern the Katsuren areas. Amawari was faithful to his king, so the king let him marry his daughter, Momotu-fumi-agari. She was a very attractive lady so her mother, the queen, sent with her, one of her own retainers, U-fu-uni-gusuku. He was to be personal bodyguard at Katsuren.

Over the years Momotu-fumi-agari fell in love with her guard. When Amawari staged his famous coup at Naka-gusuku Castle, Momotu-fumi-agari and her lover fled back to her father at Shuri. Amawari followed them there; but the King (having learned from his daughter of Amawari's treachery which had resulted in the death of Lord Gosamaru and his men) refused to open the gates to him. So Amawari attacked Shuri. He was defeated by the King's soldiers and executed.

Thus ends the story of a kind and generous boy who became a greedy and deceitful petty ruler.

Ferry   Located about 21 miles northeast of Sukiran, this
of   ferry is about 45 minutes by bus from Sukiran.
Yakena   Yakena is the doorway to the offshore islands
          of Yaby, Henza, Hamahiga, Miyagi and Ekei.
Those islands are a fine view from the Katsuren Castle site. At low tide hours you can walk to the offshore island of Henza, a distance of about 4 kilometers; sometimes the tide is so low you can drive a car from Yakena to Henza island.

Many Americans on Saturday and Sunday go to these islands for fishing. There are about 60 boats at Yakena Port which you can hire for fishing trips.

Panoramic   From the upper porch of the Fort Buckner
View   Officers' Club, there is an excellent view of
              American installations in the Sukiran area.
The small farms of Jagaru nestle below, the village itself occupying the hill between here and the highway. You get

FERRY OF YAKENA

almost an aerial view of the village and the "American scene on Okinawa." To the east are the Sukiran housing areas, the shopping area, Buckner Theater, and USARYIS Headquarters, framed by the high hills of the Nakagusuku Castle site. To the south are the Sukiran Recreational Area, troop barracks, the village of Oyama, Kuzu Peninsula, and the rugged hills of Kakazu Ridge. The Military Stockade and the new hospital are in the foreground to the west, and radio towers dot the view in the Sobe and Yomitan areas to the North. On the hillside below are examples of the two major types of tombs used on Okinawa: the "turtle-back" type and the cave type.

Tombs on Okinawa are more than a burial vault; they are works of art, valuable pieces of real estate, and temples to the spirits of family ancestors. For the most part, the tombs and burial customs on Okinawa have not been influenced either by Shintoism or Buddhism, but rather by Taoism which is related to ancestor worship. Two types of tombs are prevalent on Okinawa today: the older *hafu* (cave type) and the *kame-no-ko* (turtle-back type). The *hafu* was originally for the exclusive use of the old island nobility, but it has since been adopted by many poor people. In ancient times, the peasants of feudal Okinawa did not utilize tombs, but placed their dead in natural caves around the shores of the island. On the Jagaru hillside there are a number of cave type tombs. The poorer people use this type because they are easy to build and cost very little. As need arises, a volunteer group from the village is called together to excavate a location on a hillside.

When death occurs, a mosquito net is placed over the corpse and the room in which it rests is hung with scrolls depicting family interests, either religious or symbolic. Burial takes place within 12 to 24 hours after death, with the corpse arrayed in all the best kimonos owned during life, and other earthly possessions placed in the wooden coffin with it. Then the coffin is mounted on a litter and carried to the family tomb in a procession of mourners (sometimes including professional ones). The procession moves at a hurried pace rather than in a stately march as in the West and, in the populous centers, usually in the evening. Upon arrival at the tomb, the coffin is placed inside the tomb and the door to the tomb is then sealed with plaster or cement. During the funeral at the tomb, there is no display of emotion over the loss of the loved one because this would make his departing spirit reluctant to leave and would therefore be discourteous to the dead. Topics of ordinary conversation are discussed so that the spirit of the deceased might know that life will

FUNERAL "GAN" OR LITTER

continue the same without him; this knowledge is supposed to make the spirit less reluctant to leave this world and his family behind. Following the brief funeral, the participants go to the seashore to let the salt air and water cleanse each and everyone, chasing away the spirit of death so that it will not visit the home soon again.

These rites are repeated for three days to convince the spirit that life will continue without it and that the members of the family await its return during the O-bon season. On the fourth day, prayers are offered to the spirit to "settle down and remain at peace in its new realm". For 49 days after the funeral, the mourners return to the tomb and pray, sometimes in front of the sealed door to the tomb, sometimes in a specially built "mourning hut". Food offerings are also left at the tomb during this period.

The little picture above, shows the *gan* in which the

coffin is carried to the tomb. It is red in color, has latticed sides, and a roof like a temple with bells at the four corners. It is about three feet square because the corpse is doubled up into the pre-natal position it had in the womb. The *gan* is the property of the town and is loaned out to its citizens as occasion arises.

At present many continue to use the ancestral tombs; but cremation is now being accepted, especially in the urban areas. The ashes are preserved in very simple urns.

Kadena and Onna

Kadena. Situated on the west side of central Okinawa, the area of Kadena is about 800,000 square feet. At the present time its population is about 11,385 in 2,479 families, and 85 per cent of its land has been used as military area.

Before the Battle of Okinawa, Kadena was a farming village. The biggest sugar mill on Okinawa was located in Kadena. Most of its farming products were carried by train to Naha for sale, but now most of its people have turned to commercial firms which are growing with the patronage from U. S. bases. The village buys about 3,000 pounds of vegetables from Naha for their daily supply. This village is the birth place of Noguni Sokan, the father of the sweet potato. His monument is located just north of the Kadena Junior High School. People say that the sweet potato was first cultivated by the American Indian and introduced to Spain by Columbus. Later Mr. Noguni found it in China and he brought it to Okinawa in 1605. Then it was introduced into Kagoshima, Japan, by one of the members of the Satsuma clan which conquered Okinawa; Japanese people called it "Satsuma-imo" (Satsuma-potato).

Hiza Bashi
This bridge spans the Hiza Gawa (Bishi Gawa) which flows into the China Sea just above Kadena Circle. Many years ago, Yushiya Umichiru was sold by her parents to be trained as a geisha in Naha. Sad at leaving her home, she hoped that the high waters of the Bishi Gawa might deter her journey. But when she reached the river she found a new bridge had been built on which she

1. Noguni Sokan Monument.
2. Hiza Bashi.
3. Tako-Yama.
4. Yamada Castle Site.
5. Moon Beach.
6. Tancha Beach.
7. Manza-mo.

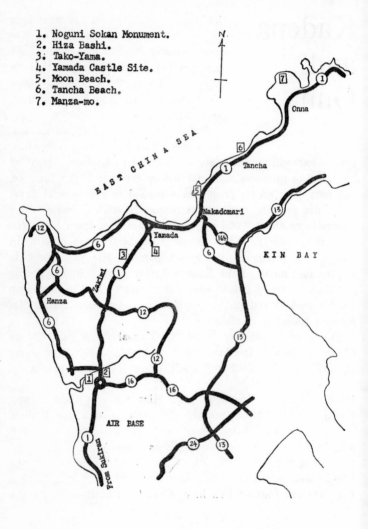

could easily cross over to the southern lands. Years later she wrote an ode to the bridge:

I resent Hiza-Bashi.

Cold-hearted men they were

Who built this bridge for me to tread on.

A modern concrete bridge has replaced the old one of stone and wood; and the site is marked by a monument and plaque at the side of the road.

O-wan   Legend says that in the village of O-wan, located just north of Hiza Bashi, there was a famous well which was shaped like a half moon, so people called it "Ama-kawa" which means "Heaven's Well". (It is in the present O-wan housing area). When a baby was born they used the water for the baby's first bath. This water cleansed the baby of all evil spirits. The general of the Satsuma clan heard the story of the well and was so interested in it that he left the Port of Unten early in the morning intent on capturing Ama-kawa. He anchored off the shore of Toguchi Port just before the sun went down over the east China Sea. Seeing the ships, the women of the village consulted together. They realized that the steep cliffs protected them from any attack from the sea, but also that they would need to protect themselves in case any soldiers landed further south and came at them from the rear. (There were evidently no men to defend Ama-kawa).

So the women decided to draw water from the well and boil it to make rice-gruel (which holds its heat). They would pour it over the hillside of Ama-kawa if Satsuma's soldiers approached. After a while the Satsuma soldiers did come from behind the Ama-kawa slope. At first the Satsuma soldiers, who did not know what was on the road, stepped into the rice-gruel and scalded their feet. (In those days they wore zori, which did not protect their feet from the hot rice-gruel). Some of Satsuma soldiers were just standing and watching the women who were on the hill busily making more rice-gruel to pour over the slope, so that the soldiers couldn't attack Ama-kawa. The General quickly reasoned that since the women poured rice-gruel on the road he couldn't make an attack on Ama-kawa. Also, he realized that his men were tired and hungry. Finally he ordered his men to eat the rice-gruel. Having thus eliminated the main blocking factor, he went on to attack Ama-kawa.

Tako-   Between Kina, in Yomitan-son and Yamada, in
yama   Onna-son, there are about 4 kilometers of winding
             road called "Tako-Yama". In olden times there
were many trees growing on both sides of the road and hills
which rise on either side. The sunshine never came through
the trees and it was dark even in the day time. In olden times
this was a barrier gate going to northern Okinawa from South
and Central Okinawa, and there were bandits who appeared
on the road and robbed travellers, but in the time of Meiji
(the 122nd Japanese Emperor who reigned during 1866-1911)
all the trees were cut down and these became bare hills.

Yamada   Yamada is located 6 miles north of Kadena Circle.
Castle   In olden times Yamada was a part of Yomitan-son,
Site   but in 1698 it became a part of Onna-son, Yamada
             Castle was located on a hill 1 kilometer east of
Yamada Village. The castle was built by the ancestors of

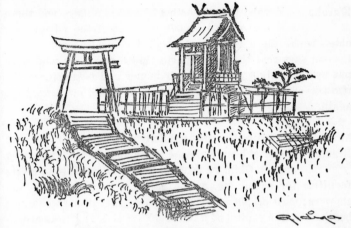

SHRINE NEAR NOGUNI SOKAN MONUMENT

Gosamaru (Gosamaru is the man who built Nakagusuku Castle) and they lived here for many generations; but after Okinawa was united, Gosamaru moved Yamada Castle to Zakimi, in Yomitan-son. When he moved the castle to Zakimi, many people came to him and wished to help him because he was the most highly respected of all people in Okinawa. There were no trucks for transporting the stones; they were passed from hand to hand along a line of villagers stretching from Yamada to Zakimi, a distance of 5 kilometers. This method of transporting was very common in those days; it is called "Te-watashi" (hand to hand). At the present time there is nothing attractive to the people who visit there; but Gosamaru's ancestors' tomb is on the old castle site and reminds us of what this hill was in olden times.

Kuraha   Kuraha is just north of Yamada Village and there
          is a nice sandy beach in front of the village.   In
olden times there was a hotel called "Kuraha-Sundunuchi".
Legend says that this hotel master killed travellers who were
put up for a night and took their money and possessions.   So
if a traveller stayed in the hotel once, he would not come back
again.

Moon   According to the publicity attending its opening
Beach   the most beautiful sand beach and the best swimming
          spot on Okinawa is Moon Beach.   There are complete
facilities for swimming, a fine restaurant, game room, and
showers; most people who visit there say that it is a wonderful
beach.   With a capital of ¥10,000,000 ($85,000) it was organ-
ized in 1956 by Mr. Heshikiya, who as president of the firm,
visited Hawaii, Hong Kong, and Japan to investigate their
tourist facilities.   It was completed in June 1957; cost of
construction was $150,000 and its area is 580 sq. ft.   It is
located 9 miles north of Kadena Circle and was opened in
July 1957.   At that time it was not very popular with the
Okinawans because the admission of ¥30 ($.25) was too
expensive for a community to which many beaches without
charge were available.   Next year they reorganized the facilities and admission dropped from ¥30 to ¥10; that summer
there were many Americans and Okinawans enjoying it in
good friendship.   It was named "Moon Beach" because, when
seen from off the shore, it has the shape of a half moon.

Tancha   This village is famous for the folk dance song of
          "Tancha-me-nu".   It was composed by chiefs of
three villages about 110 years ago as a welcome to King Sho-

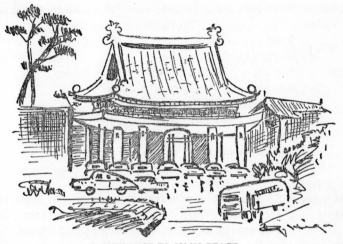

ENTRANCE TO MOON BEACH

Tai on his Kunigami tour (Northern Okinawa). At that time there were no dance songs in the three villages with which to entertain the king; so they decided to compose a dance song representing the fishermen's village of Tancha. It is danced on the stage usually by a boy and a girl dressed in clothes of banana fiber; the boy has an oar on his shoulder, the girl a bamboo basket in her hand. They dance nimbly to the accompaniment of the samisen. It became very popular because a Japanese motion picture company made a movie called "Lily Tower" in 1953 in which a group of girls were gathered together singing and dancing "Tancha-me-nu". A western piano accompaniment was composed by Kikuko Kanai in 1953 for use in the picture. The steps of the dance are simple and the rhythm of the music so regular, that young moderns of

Okinawa have included it in their evenings of western square
dancing. The words of "Tancha-me-nu" are below:

> They say many Suru-gua (small fish) come
> To the shores of Tancha
> But those who fish its waters
> Know a finer fish is caught there
> The Yamatu Misum (sardines).
> The fisher-boy fills his boat
> From his nets.
> And gives his catch to the girl
> To sell.

Manza- Along the coral upheaval, located north of Onna in
Mo   1726, King Sho-Kei came by dropping in on his
        tour around Kunigami (northern part of Okinawa).
He said that the place was wide enough for ten thousand
people to be seated, and thus they say that it was named
"Manza-Mo" meaning "Ten thousand seats". The famous
Ryukyuan poetess, Onna Nabe, made a poem in honor of the
king on that occasion. Roughly it goes as follows:

> Halt your roaring, Waves!
> Halt your blowing, too, Winds!
> For this is the day
> To welcome our king from Shuri.

In the pine forest nearby, a monument with an inscription of
Nabe's is found.

Central Okinawa: Koza to Kin

The City of Koza.   Koza is located in the center of Okinawa and its area is about 1,144,000 square feet. In 1957 its population was about 50,000 in 10,000 families.   About 72% of its area has been used by the American military; 65% of the townspeople are engaged in retail business. The many foreigners visiting the city are estimated at 5,000 to 10,000 per day.

Koza is the second largest and newest city in the Ryukyus, a postwar boom town which is growing rapidly. Koza has boomed because of the presence of American military bases nearby and the resultant spending of U.S. servicemen in its restaurants, clubs, theaters, and souvenir shops.   No one knows better the benefits of the American serviceman's business than do the individual citizens of Koza whose daily bread they supply.

Undoubtedly the one city in the Ryukyus most dependent on American business, Koza would lose most of its population and crumble into dust in the classical American frontier manner if its American patronage was withdrawn.   Koza has no other important source of income.   Each city and town in the Ryukyus has its own particular character; but an attempt to grasp the character of Koza is an attempt to grasp a handful of smoke for Koza's character is both blatant and elusive at the same time.   Koza is a six-year-old girl; what kind of woman will she grow up to be?   Right now she is a boom town reminiscent of the American frontier as

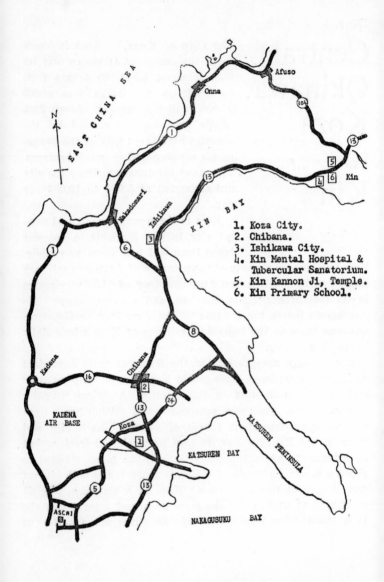

1. Koza City.
2. Chibana.
3. Ishikawa City.
4. Kin Mental Hospital &
   Tubercular Sanatorium.
5. Kin Kannon Ji, Temple.
6. Kin Primary School.

depicted in the movies. The bright façades, the dark back streets, the lack of public utilities and paved streets are all typical of a boom town. Also typical is the fact that a lot of money changes hands in Koza, most of it from American to Ryukyuan hands; and small fortunes have been made and lost there.

The site of today's Koza was formerly only farmland except for the prewar sub-villages of Kamahara and Murokawa. Kamahara was just a few houses west of the present Highway 24 on the hill leading from the present central business section to Koza four corners; Murokawa was slightly east on the same hill. Ten years ago there were no home sites at the present intersection of Highways 24 and 13; in 1952-53 it was still only a dusty, smoky village of thatched roofs that was beginning to spread out along the new roads to what is today the central business area and Shimabuku to the south, Chibana to the northeast, and Awase to the east.

The construction of military bases and modern highways brought to Koza many people whose livelihood was directly or indirectly dependent on Americans. Quite a few of today's citizens moved to Koza from Ishikawa when free U.S. military transportation was discontinued for Ryukyuan employees of U.S. bases. (There are 5,000 U.S. employees living in Koza). Others came from all over the Ryukyus; in fact, from all over the world. Some of Koza's leading business men, for example, returned to Okinawa after living and working in the United States for many years.

Most of the citizens of Koza are making money—real money. It takes searching to find a house today without a tile roof and most of them are painted as well. East of the central business district is an attractive residential section which

is comparable to any on Okinawa.   It is paradoxically true that
both the most and least attractive buildings in Koza are its
business places.   And it is unusual, to Americans at least,
that many of Koza's businessmen have invested more in their
homes than in the business places.   Perhaps the most modern
and attractive buildings in Koza are the post office and central
telephone exchange, both of which were completed with U.S.
financial aid. The annual contest in store construction and merchandise display, sponsored by the Merchants' Association
since 1956, is creating more attractive retail establishments.

Actually there are several Kozas.   There is Shimabuku,
the central business section formerly known as New Koza,
and Koza Four Corners.   The Shimabuku section along Highway 24 probably presents the most attractive front with its
souvenir shops selling almost every tangible thing an American
might want, but very few things the average Ryukyuan would
use.   Behind Highway 24, which cuts the city in two length-
wise, are many shops catering to Ryukyuans; but one has to
look for them.   The central business area, particularly Airbase
Street and Koza Center main street, is lined with blocks of
clubs, restaurants, and pawn shops.   Some of the better clubs
have sunken dance floors.   Patronage is 99% American; it is
a rare occasion when a Ryukyuan customer comes in.   The
Koza Four Corners section is primarily devoted to Ryukyuan
business and there is a noticeable lack of souvenir shops.
Bars catering to American trade fringe the section, especially
along Highway 13; but emphasis in this section is not on
American trade.

Chibana   Chibana was famous for its pottery about 260
                 years ago.   The design of the pottery was a

very simple one which was said to show European influence. Legend says that a man came from China to teach Ryukyuans how to make the clay-tile roof.   He fell in love with a woman of the town and asked her to marry him; but she refused telling him she was already a married woman.   He took his request to the king of the Ryukyus saying, "If she does not marry me, I will not teach your people how to make a tile." Whereupon the King ordered her to abandon her husband and marry the man from China.   After her marriage to him, she wrote this poem:

> "I am standing on a red tile roof
> And looking down south
> Where my loved one is;
> I can see my husband's village,
> But I cannot see my husband."

The City of Ishikawa   Facing the Pacific Ocean, the area of Ishikawa is 857,500 square feet, and in 1956 its population was 17,346 in 3,593 families.   The principal occupations at that time were: Farming, 1,430 families; commercial firms, 520 families; U.S. employed, 400 families.   Before the Battle of Okinawa, Ishikawa was a village of 1,800 persons; its population soared to more than 30,000 by August 1945.   By 1946 it was the largest city on Okinawa; ten years later its population of 17,346 made it the fifth largest.

The rapid rise of Ishikawa's population was the result of many factors.   Immediately after the war a detention camp was established nearby.   Some of the persons who lived in the camp were residents of the Naha-Shuri area who fled north of the main battle; many obtained employment with the military and civil governments which were established at Ishikawa immediately after the battle.

When the military and civil governments moved to Chinen, many of the people followed their jobs; others of them returned to their homes in Naha. When free U.S. military transportation was discontinued for Ryukyuan workers at U.S. bases, more people left Ishikawa to be nearer their places of employment. Thus Ishikawa's population dropped. In 1957 it was again on the rise as the result of U.S. Marine camps being built in the neighborhood.

Because it was once located in their city, the people of Ishikawa feel a strong kinship with the government of the Ryukyus. They are also more interested in the cultural aspects of life than in material gain, and are proud that the city purchased the site of the Ryukyuan-American Information Center so that it might be preserved for posterity as a cultural asset to the community.

Ishikawa's streets are not paved and most of its commercial buildings are not more than two-story wooden structures. It has three large theaters; most of its business stems from the fact that it is the major shopping center in northeast Okinawa. It becomes a "resort town" in summer for the American crowds at Ishikawa Beach.

Kin   The gateway to northern Okinawa, Kin Village
Village   has a population of 6,885, and is 3,734 *chobu*
              (30,366,000 square feet) in area. In prewar days
it was a rich community with large remittances from emigrants in Hawaii and the Philippines. After the war it became a poor village as most of its farmland was occupied by U.S.

KANNON TEMPLE NEAR KIN

forces and remittances from abroad have fallen off. It is the birthplace of Mr. Kyuzo Toyama, the father of Okinawan emigration. It escaped war damage.

Kin Mental Hospital and Tubercular Sanatorium
This institution completed in May 1953 with financial assistance from GRI and USCAR; cost of construction was $35,800. There are 70 beds for mental patients; it is estimated that about 1,000 persons need treatment in such an institution. The tubercular sanatorium has 200 beds; the estimated number of tubercular patients needing hospitalization is 5,000. Most of these are out-patients who recuperate at home assisted by government funds.

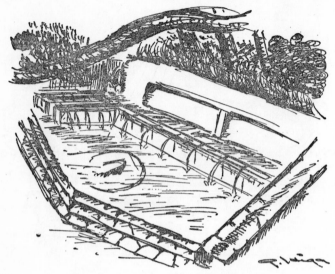

KIN WELLS AND NATURAL SPRING BATHS

Kannon   Situated on the west side of Kin Village the Kan-
Temple   nonji is one of the oldest on Okinawa.   On the
          temple grounds, is the greatest stalactite grotto
in Okinawa.   In 1522 a Japanese priest, Nisshu, arrived in the
port of Tomikura near Kin Village.   In those days, a huge
serpent lived in this grotto inflicting injuries on the villagers.
The priest drove the serpent and all the evil spirits out, saving
the people from further injury.   He then established this
temple.   Having a good harvest in the year of the priest's
coming, the people sang in praise of him saying, "a living
god has come to us and changed white sands into polished
rice".   The temple was of the Zen sect, but was converted to

KIN ELEMENTARY SCHOOL

the Shingon sect in the reign of Sho Shitsu. The temple and grotto stand today as they did in olden times.

If you step into the cave, you will find it quite cool. To the right of the third step as you enter, you can see a model of a Buddhist temple (size 4 feet by ½ feet). This is *Sente Kannon* which means "Temple of a Thousand Hands". The thousand hands represent the willingness of the deity to help you if you have any troubles or special wishes.

Shall we step into the cave further? There is a long way to go. Many people who visit this cave want to know where it ends; but none has yet found out. There are 22 passage-ways all going in various directions. One passage-way is 220

meters long and emerges behind the Kin Public Building.
Another, about 100 meters to the right, is unexplored beyond
its first 1500 meters. At this point a stream was discovered
in which many eels and lobsters live. Legend says that a dog
put into this cave was later found on Kudaka-shima, an offshore
island in the Pacific. Here adventures await the explorer; will
you be the one to solve this mystery of the Kin caves?

Kin   The wells and baths of spring form another inter-
Wells   esting spot to visit in this village. They are used
and   for bathing and for washing. Surrounded by
Natural   shrubs and flowers, and fed by a mountain spring
Spring   of crystal clear water, they are reported to be
Baths   the envy of every other village on Okinawa. The
             well-baths were designed by the local patriot,
Kyuzo Toyama, who later led the first Okinawan emigrants
to Hawaii. His monument, erected by a devoted people stands
on a hill just north of Kin Kannonji Temple. From the hill
on which it stands, there is a beautiful view of low hills,
extensive rice paddies, and the Pacific Ocean with the mounds
of the offshore islands limiting the view at the horizon.

The road from the foot of this hill leads past the rice fields
to Kin Beach which is much favored by skin-divers.

Kin   Unique as the first of its kind on Okinawa Kin
Elementary   Elementary School was also a testimony to
School   the high economic level of the old town. Many
             of the emigrants who left Okinawa became
permanent residents and citizens of the United States and
South American countries.They prospered in their new home-
lands and sent much money to their relatives on Okinawa,

thus making Kin a rich village. As a result of this bounty, the people of Kin built this two-story concrete school in 1925. It has a bell in its tower and, unlike many new postwar schools, it has attractive landscaping and a beautiful garden. It stands today as originally erected.

Iha Castle Site On Highway 6 just north of Iha Village there once stood a castle. It was the castle of Iha Anjo who lived about 480 years ago (1478). His tomb is to the north of the site. This is one of the eight beauty spots of Okinawa and is a good place for a family picnic on a hot summer day. On this high hill you are cooled by fresh ocean breezes as you look down over Ishikawa City and Ishikawa Beach, across the tea plantations on the hillside to the rice paddies along the low shore, and on to the offshore islands in the Pacific Ocean.

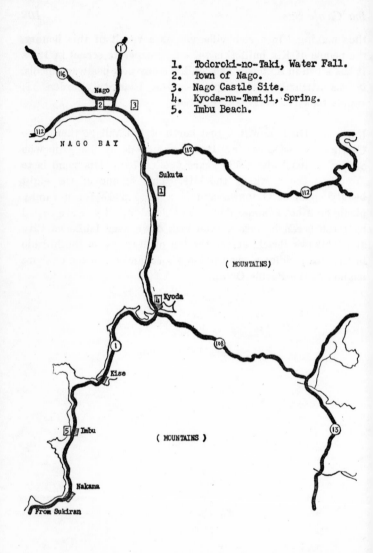

1. Todoroki-no-Taki, Water Fall.
2. Town of Nago.
3. Nago Castle Site.
4. Kyoda-nu-Temiji, Spring.
5. Imbu Beach.

NAGO BAY

Nago

Sukuta

(MOUNTAINS)

Kyoda

Kise

Imbu

(MOUNTAINS)

Nakama

From Sukiran

Nago: Portal to the North

This tour follows Highway 13 along the Pacific Ocean, through Kin to Matsuda. Just beyond Matsuda, we turn west on Highway 108, crossing the mountains to Kyoda on the East China Sea, and proceeding north to Nago on Highway 1.

Todoroki-no-Taki. This is the first of many waterfalls to be seen as you proceed north into the mountains. It is located about 500 meters south of Sukuta Village on Highway 1. From the crest of the falls, between two huge rocks about 15 meters high, the water rushes and tumbles down, making a roaring sound. It presents an impressive sight; and the boulders at its base form a popular place for cooling and relaxing on a hot summer day.

Nago-cho This city is 68 kilometers north of Naha—a two-hour bus ride along the beaches and high cliffs that border the East China Sea. It was a sizeable town in prewar days; with a concentration of government agencies, schools, banks, and commercial firms, it was the northern center of politics, culture, and trade. The town extends for 2 kilometers along Nago Bay, which is encompassed by Mount Katsuo, Mount Onna, and Mount Nago. The sea waters of this sheltered bay are as calm as a lake. The climate here is mild and the area is one of the best summer resort locations and watering places on Okinawa. The main north-south highway passes through the center of the town and continues north to the tip of Okinawa; Highway 112 leaves the town center for a detour around Motobu Peninsula. Two bus companies provide frequent and reliable transportation around the peninsula; and Nago is the terminus for the bus lines running north and south from here.

Although the largest rice plantation on Okinawa is located just north of Nago, most of the farming in the immediate area is dry land type. Forest products are firewood and lumber. Fishing includes the usual offshore varieties, whaling and the unique porpoise round-up.

The porpoise round-up combines an industrial pursuit and a village ceremony. Large groups of porpoise visit Nago Bay between March and May in the lunar calendar. At this time, all the people in the town take off from their tasks, the schools close, and all the able men go out in a fleet of boats commanded by the Mayor of Nago. Each man brings his own oar and whatever weapon he chooses. When the porpoises come close enough to catch, the Mayor lowers his flag. This is the signal to start, and the battle between men and porpoises begins. As spears and knives flash and clubs swing, the blue sea waters turn pink and red; and on the shore, the heap of porpoises grows larger until the white sandy beach is almost completely covered with the catch. That night all the housewives prepare special food; the families pray to their ancestors and petition the god of the sea that the porpoises will visit Nago Bay again next year. In a year when there is a large catch, the Mayor who commanded the catching is almost sure of re-election. If the catch is small, the Mayor will probably lose in the next election. So the porpoise round-up at Nago is a sort of "primary" for the mayoral election which follows it.

TODOROKI-NO-TAKI

Whaling has been done by the fishermen of Nago for many years, but failed to develop as an industry because there were no efficient processing or preserving facilities in the town. Since the war, improved methods and the facilities of a modern whaling station have eliminated the necessity of immediate consumption of the catch and whaling is becoming a profitable industry for the people of Nago.

Nago's business places generally display a greater variety

of consumer goods such as motorcycles, hardware, house furnishings, electrical appliances, books, and magazines than other towns of the same size (1955 population: 16,069). The number and variety of books and magazines goes along with the town's pride in its well kept and well run schools.

Tourists are usually interested in Nago's open-air market place which is located just off the main street. Set under large canopies which shield it from the sun, the market has two main sections: food in one, clothing, household goods, and toys in the other. The merchandise here is designed for Okinawan consumption, not the tourist trade. While many of the foods on display look strange and may not be palatably tempting, they afford a fascinating insight to local customs; and, in season, the delicate aroma of ripe pineapple from the peninsula farms is a mouth-watering reminder that the "good earth" grows much the same things in the same climate around the world.

In recent years, Nago has become conscious of the tourist trade as have her sister cities in the south, and businesses of this nature are opening up. One of the first of these is the $50,000 Kyokan Hotel completed in 1956. Rated by some as the finest hotel in the Ryukyus, it is a three-story, concrete building with 24 rooms equally divided between Oriental and Western styles. The large, airy suites combine the best of both cultures and offer the guest some of the finest scenery on Okinawa. From the roof of the hotel, there is an excellent view of Nago and its environs.

Nago   The site of Nago Castle is on a hill 1 kilometer
Castle   southeast of the town of Nago. About 800 years
Site   ago, the castle was occupied by a leader of the

NAGO CASTLE SITE

people named Tenson-shi. The community of Nago developed around the castle and many of the present residents trace their descent from Tenson. When the lord of Nakijin rose to power, control over the Nago area was moved to his castle, Hokuzan. The *anji* (lord) of Nago became a vassal of the Nakijin *anji*. This relationship irked the Nago *anji* and revolt was constantly threatening. To ensure control over Nago, the last ruler of Hokuzan Castle took the second son of the Nago *anji* as a hostage. This added fuel to the fire; so, when King Sho-Hashi from Shuri attacked Hokuzan Castle, the local lords of Nago, Haneji, and Kunigami joined forces with him to destroy Hokuzan Castle. Following their victory,

the first son of the Nago *anji* went to Shuri as one of the
king's retainers and the castle succeeded to the second son.

At the present time there is nothing of interest at the old
castle site; but if you climb up to the top of the hill, there
is a fine view over the whole of the Nago area and Nago Bay.
You may also see the newly planted cherry trees, and, in
the right season, the festive beauty of their blossoms.

Kyoda-nu-   A pleasant stop on the way back from Nago
Temiji   is about 200 meters east of Kyoda Bay and
                 is the scene of one of Okinawa's widely known
legends: "Many years ago, a traveller passing this spot
was very thirsty. He came to the spring and wished to drink
the water, but he had no cup. As he stood there, perplexed,
a young maiden appeared and, cupping her hands under the
spring, offered him the chance to slake his thirst. Refreshed
by the cool water he continued on his journey, but returned
here to meet her again; and, in the end they were married."

Imbu   After Moon Beach was built, there was a "com-
Beach   mercial beaches boom" along the coasts of Okinawa;
             and people began to fear that there would soon be
no beach where one could go swimming without paying a
fee. Imbu is a beach where there is still no charge. It is
located about 10 miles north of Moon Beach. Moon Beach is
a man-made attraction, but Imbu Beach is a natural beauty
because there are about 200 shade trees standing along the
1500 meters of white sandy shore. Imbu is operated by the
Nakama Village Office. The village chief says they planted
about 350 trees instead of erecting buildings which would
spoil the natural beauty. Nakama Village offers the people

a chance to relax under the shadow of the trees on their summer holidays without a fee so that anyone can enjoy the waters and the shade of Imbu Beach.

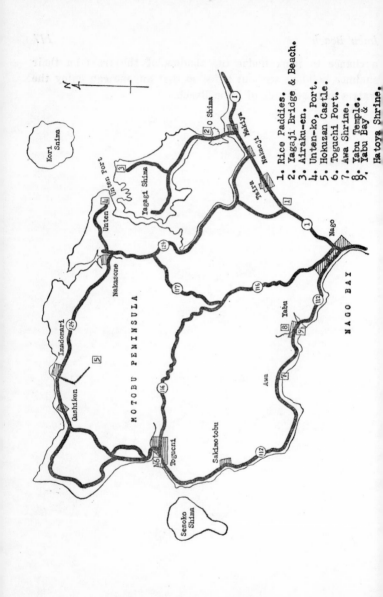

1. Rice Paddies.
2. Yagaji Bridge & Beach.
3. Airaku-en.
4. Unten-ko, Port.
5. Hokuzan Castle.
6. Toguchi Port.
7. Awa Shrine.
8. Yabu Temple.
9. Yabu Bay &
   Hatoya Shrine.

Motobu Peninsula

Haneji Rice Paddies. Located about 4 kilometers northeast of Nago, along Highway 1, these rice paddies are the second largest on Okinawa; their area is about 1,600,000 square feet, and their yearly produce is valued at 3,000,000 yen ($25,000). These rice paddies belong to the people of Haneji-son. Haneji-son is composed of 16 villages near the rice paddies, and its population is 9,927 in 2,134 families.

Yagaji Island   At the mouth of Unten Port in Haneji Bay is Yagaji Island measuring 19,635 kilometers in perimeter. In prewar days, it belonged municipally to Haneji-son; but, after the war, it became an independent *son* (village). Its population is 3,915 in 577 families, and its main products are sugar, salt, and potatoes. The canoes, or jolly-boats, were the only available means of communication with the mainland, until two reinforced concrete bridges were completed with the financial help (to the amount of 15,000,000 yen) from GRI, and the volunteer labor service rendered by islanders. The one bridge between O-shima and Okinawa proper is called "Haneji O-bashi," and is 200 feet in length. The other, between O-shima and Yagaji Island, is called "Yagaji Grand Bridge," (480 feet in length and 16 feet in width). The bridges are passable for busses, and cars; islanders now have easy access to the islands, and many people who have cars spend the hot summer holidays at Yagaji beach.

Airaku-en   The "Garden of Love and Comfort" is the name of the government supported leprosarium on the

western end of Yagaji Island. It was established by the
Japanese government in November, 1938. Most of the 900
patients are active in the work of the colony—farming,
fishing, tending stock, and caring for the acute cases being
treated in a 40-bed hospital.

Unten   This port lies at the northeast end of Nakijin-son,
Port   between Shimo-Unten and Yagaji Island, a distance
              of about 3 kilometers from the village of Nakasone
on Highway 124. Commanding a fine prospect, it is a good
port in the northern district, as the sea within is deep. This
place is famous as the landing spot of Minamoto-no-Tametomo
(Shoe Son became the first king of a united Okinawa) and a
monument is founded in his honor with a letter written thereon
by Admiral Togo of the Japanese navy. When the Satsuma
forces made their inroads on Okinawa in the Keicho era in
March, 1610, they were first beaten off at Naha Port. They
succeeded in penetrating into Okinawa from this port of
Unten and taking Shuri by assault through Nago. Moreover,
this port is used for the port of shelter in case of typhoons
because of the cliff's holes which protect it from the open sea.
At the foot of the cliff, northeast side of the peninsula, there
are 13 old tombs in which skeletons lay in heaps. These tombs
are called *momojana*. People say these bones were soldiers
of Okinawa and Satsuma. When Satsuma attacked Okinawa,
Unten was a hard fought site of the Keicho battle in 1610,
so they lost many soldiers at this place. After the war the
people collected these bones and buried them at this spot. But
some people say the bones are those of King Sho-toku's
retainers who were destroyed by King Sho-en in 1470. There
is another tomb which has no entrance. The people say it is

HOKUZAN CASTLE SITE

the tomb of one of the king's family who was a heavy saké drinker. The people made his tomb without a mouth so the spirit could not come out for the offerings of food and drink which are customarily carried to the tomb of the departed.

Unten Tunnel — The tunnel is the approach to Unten Port. It was constructed in November 1924; its length is 48 feet and its width is 18 feet. It is the third largest tunnel on Okinawa.

Hokuzan Castle Site — Situated on a high hill about 2 kilometers southeast of Imadomari Village on Highway 124, this particular site has a long history. The first castle on this site was built in 950 AD by the

YABU KANNON-DO

local lord or *anji*. It was called Nakijin Castle after the district over which it ruled.

The district became a dependency of Shunten who united all of Okinawa under one rule in 1187. This relationship continued until shortly after Tamagusuku ascended the throne at the age of 19. Under the misrule of this young and sensuous king, the United Kingdom collapsed. At that time a lord of the Hokuzan sovereignty seized Nakijin Castle and established himself there as ruler of northern Okinawa including Yoron, Okierabu, Iheya, and Izena Islands. The name, Hokuzan, dates from this time. The castle site is 65 meters above sea level, its border is on the steep cliff with scenic attractions. It is 1,100 meters in circumference

AWA SHRINE

and 19,900 square meters in area. Although the gates and walls were partly destroyed, they never fail to remind one of the old castle. On the site there is a sanctuary, several old stone lanterns, and two monuments; one is inscribed with names of the lords of Nakijin Castle; the other, with the letters "Sanhoku, Nakijin Castle" written by Admiral Togo of the Japanese navy. Just east of the latter there is a rock which is fenced in by a stone wall. It was erected to the guardian angel of the castle. When the castle fell, the master of the castle was vexed and with his sword cut off the stone, which he erected as a castle god. He then killed himself. The castle site was owned by the Nakijin family until the time of Meiji (1866-1911), but now it is under the administration of the village office of Imadomari. A driveway up the mountain has been completed for visitors, making the castle gate accessible by car; there is a parking lot, lavatory and cold drink stand. The new stone steps were constructed in June 1958 with GRI financial assistance. Before the battle of Okinawa, the Hokuzan Castle site was more attractive than the Nakagusuku Castle site. More people visited at Nakijin Castle site but at present the castle site itself has nothing attractive to offer because the castle walls are completely covered with grass. At the top of the hill, however, there is a very nice view over the village of Imadomari and the offshore islands.

Nakijin-son   Composed of 16 local villages along Highway 124 the population of Nakijin-son is about 13,775 in 2,813 families and its yearly income is about $137,500. Pine trees grow on both sides of Highway 124 and the old streets are about 180 years old. Most of the trees on Okinawa were blown up in the last war. Those at Nakijin are the oldest trees growing here on Okinawa.

Toguchi   Also called "Tsu-guchi" meaning "port-entry", this is the fishing port town located at the mouth of the Mitsuna River. It is the second largest town in Kunigami (northern) district and a police station, a fishing school, shipyards, and firms are located there. It is 20 kilometers from Nago, and busses are available in between. Motorboats ply busily between this port and the isolated islands, such as Ie-shima, Iheya-shima and Izena. It is also the trading center of fishing and agricultural products. Behind this town stand steep hills and before it, the Minna and Ie-shima Islands are seen vividly in the sea. The water is as calm as that of an inland sea and is especially beautiful towards sunset.

Yabu   This temple is to be found about 300 meters
Kannon-do   northeast of Yabu Village on Highway 112,
                a distance of about 34 miles north of Sukiran.
It is not clear when it was erected, but judging from the letters on the old stone in the yard, it was first erected about 400 years ago. The legend of the temple is as follows: In olden times there was an old *akamata* (snake) that had transformed himself into a handsome boy and had tempted the farmer's daughter in the village. A famous priest, Ryu-un-washo, came from Enkaku-ji, a temple in Shuri and made an incantation and saved the farmer's daughter from *akamata*'s temptation. So the village people respected the god of Buddha and a temple. The Buddha statues on the temple shelf were brought from Kagoshima, Japan about 300 years ago. The old temple was destroyed in the last war, and the new temple was built in September 1957 with the contributions collected from the villagers.

Awa   In the village of Awa on Highway 112 about 35
Shrine   miles north of Sukiran is a picturesque shrine.
                There are three stones dedicated to a village god
such as most villages on Okinawa have.

1. Utofui-Iwa.
2. Shioya-Bay.
3. Morikawa-nu-shi.
4. Naka-no-yama Park.
5. Huge Tree.
6. Kanamaru-ga, well.
7. Kannucha-nu-Hama, Beach.
8. Kushi Kannondo, Temple.
9. Kushi Young Lord's Tomb.

Shioya Bay and Kushi-son

The northern part of Okinawa has no historically interesting spots, but it contains the most scenically beautiful locations on the island, commanding a fine view of the China Sea and Yagaji-shima as you go north. It is worth going slowly to see the blue ocean and green hills, while driving up to Shioya Bay, across the island via Route No. 4, and south on Route No. 13 to Sukiran. On both sides of Route No. 13 the villages of Kushi-son stretch for 14 miles; you can see in them the real life of the Okinawan.

Utu-Fui-Iwa This lies about 2 kilometers off the shore from Genka Village in Haneji-son, a distance of about 12 kilometers northeast of Nago. In olden times, Okinawan young people were not allowed to select whom they wished to marry; marriages were arranged by parents. This rock takes its name from the story of a young girl who attempted to defy this custom. Her parents had insisted on her marrying a man she did not know; after the marriage she refused to live with him. So the parents put the young couple in a boat, rowed out to this rock, and left them there. For long hours, they stood on opposite sides of the rock without speaking to one another. When the sun set, the air became very cold and the man, sensing the girl's discomfort, took off his kimono and put it around her shoulders. The girl was touched by his kind gesture of protecting her and ashamed of herself for having refused to live with him. They returned to a happy life together and the rock was called a "love-making rock". (Literally: "husband-exerting-power rock".)

Shioya   Miyagi-shima (2 kilometers in perimeter) lies at
Bay   the mouth of the bay located 20 kilometers north-
          east of Nago, protecting the inland sea from the
wind and waves. The green hills of Nakayama are mirrored in the sea and it is really an enchanting view. In olden times, ferryboats plied between Shirahama and Shioya. But now, busses run on the road constructed along the coastline through Taiho and Taminato, and one can enjoy the fine scenery better. On the high hill of the Shioya to the north side of the bay, you will notice the steps going up the hill and will see a small square cement house. It is dedicated to a village god which protects village people, and this place is one of eight scenic spots on Okinawa. Just above the small house you will see a stone monument about 5 feet high. It was erected by the *Ryukyuan Shimpo* newspaper company because of the beauty of the bay.

Nakano-   This stands on the east side of a high hill in
Yama-   Shioya Village. There are about 130 steps going
Park   up the hill to the top from behind the Shioya
          public hall. On the hill top there are two monu-
ments to those killed in action in the Chinese-Japanese War and World War II. From the hill top there is a very nice view over Shioya bay, Miyagi-shima, and other offshore islands. Busses run between Nago and Hentona which pass through Shioya every 25 minutes; so you can go there by bus and enjoy the scenic tour on your holidays.

SHIOYA BAY

Shrine
of
Morikawa-
no-Shi

Located in the village of Tsuha in Ogimi-son
on Highway 1, a distance of about 52 miles
north of Sukiran, this is dedicated to the au-
thor of Ryukyuan musical play *Hana-ure-en*
(An Affair of Love). The hero of the play is the
son of one of the peers of Shuri. It is not clear why he fled
from Shuri without telling his wife or son, but he came to
the village of Tsuha and was earning his living making salt.
Later, his wife left Shuri and, disguised as a flower-seller,
set out to seek him. In her travels, she met people who told
her that the man who was making salt in Tsuha had come

SHRINE OF MORIKAWA-NO-SHI

from Shuri. She recites this poem on hearing about the salt maker:

> "I do not know where the village of Tsuha is;
> I only rely on the indication of way in my heart.
> On the journey seeking my husband.
> My sleeves are wet with the tears I have shed."

The way her heart indicated was right and they finally met in the village of Tsuha. So ends the play based on a true story. The people in the village of Tsuha revered this hero as the father of salt-making in their town and built a shrine on the original site of his house.

2000-Meter Great Wall

As we drive along Route 4, connecting Route 1 and Route 13, we can see off the left and right the white walls which follow the hill contours.

THE OLD PINE TREE

These are fences which keep away the wild boars from the pineapple plantations.

Wild boar hunting is a sport enjoyed by natives and visitors in this section. Hunting trips to this area may be arranged through USARYIS Special Services.

The
Old
Pine
Tree
When you drive on the highways, north of Kadena you will notice the old pine trees growing on both sides of the road. These trees were planted by the great 18th-century governor of Ryukyus, Mr. Saion (see Yomochi shrine). The tree in our illustration is growing on Highway 13 not very far from the village of Taira in Higashi-son. This passage from Dr. Egbert's book explains the importance of pine trees:—"Native in the Ryukyus only from Akuseki Island southward, sometimes culti-

vated in Formosa where P. taiwanensis Hayata is the principal pine. It is found wild and cultivated, especially at lower
elevations as invader of open areas and in second-growth
forests and along seashores. It grows in open stands and
singly almost everywhere. It's wood is second-grade, easily
warps and is often attacked by termites; but it is fairly resis-
tant to decay under water. This is probably the most
conspicuous and distinctive tree of Okinawa Island, at least
in the more open southern parts. As an ornamental and
shade tree it is hardly surpassed, the beauty of the open
parklike groves at Manza-mo in Okinawa being well known.
Its hardiness and rapid growth makes it specially important for reforestation and for wind-breaks and shade
trees. It readily invades disturbed land such as roadside cuts,
hence is useful in soil erosion control along with other plants.
The wood is used for outdoor construction, making mortars,
troughs, cheaper furniture and implements, and for fuel and
charcoal, for which purposes it is widely planted. Resin is
distilled from the wood and roots."

Kanamaru-ga   This is on the eastern side of Tema Village
                   on Highway 13. When Sho-Kanamaru was
driven away from Izena Island and came to this spot he fell
in love with a maiden who drew water from this well and
they were married. After this romance the village people named
it Kanamaru-ga in honor of the boy who later became king.

The   The only one of its kind here on Okinawa.
Drawbridge   The bridge connects the old village of Kade-
of   karubara and the village of Tema. It was
Tema   built in June 1957 with agriculture promotion

KANUCHA BEACH

funds from GRI. From on the bridge there is a very nice view over the small bay of Tema to the west. The bay within is so small that it looks like a river, and the sea water extends about one and a half kilometers into the village. To the east of the bridge you will see a forest in which there is a shrine.

Kanucha Beach
In Kushi-son, which stretches for 14 miles, there are several beautiful beaches for people who want to spend a hot summer holiday at the seashore. The Kanucha beach located between the village of Tema and Abu on Highway 13, is famous for the love song of "Tema-to". The village's most beautiful girl, Marumi-kana, fell in love with Kamiya who came from Shuri as a salesman. The young boys of the village were jealous of this romance because the man who came from Shuri was nice-looking compared to the boys in the farming village of Tema. They composed the song, "Tema-to", trying to chase Kamiya

away from the village and sang it loudly everywhere in the village. They hoped to make the village people inquisitive about the romance and so induce Kamiya to leave the village of Tema. They were successful and Marumi-kana was be-trothed by her parents to one of the village boys.

Fukugi   Most of the houses in the village of Tema are
Trees   fenced with the Fukugi trees; some of them are
             about 20 to 30 feet in height. Dr. Egbert H.
Walker's book "Important Trees of the Ryukyu Islands" say
that the Fukugi tree, so common on Okinawa, is not positively
related to any commonly known species. However, it resembles
a tree native to the Indian peninsula called *Garcinia Spicata*.
The Fukugi is an evergreen with gray to blackish smooth,
thick bark. Its numerous branches tend to grow upward close
to the trunk somewhat like the poplar. The leaves are
smooth, thick, and leathery like the magnolia. It bears a
small yellowish flower in the spring and a firm, fleshy fruit
in the fall. Its yellowish, hard, close-grained wood is used
as second-grade building timber. A yellow dye, obtained
from the gum which exudes from the bark, is used as an
artist's pigment (it is the source of the yellow color in the
Okinawan *bingata* prints), and also as a medicine. The
principal use of this tree, however, is as a village shade tree,
fire protection, and wind break. Abandoned village sites may
be recognized from the remaining Fukugi trees and their age
may be determined from the size of these trees.

Kushi-   Located on the Highway 13, a distance of about
son   30 miles northeast of Sukiran, its population is
             about 7,076 people forming 1200 families (about

300 are employed by the construction companies for the building of Marine bases, and come from everywhere on Okinawa). When the American military announced the building of a permanent Marine camp in Henoko Village in 1956, Henoko appeared on the top line of newspapers every day, so the people who never heard of larger Kushi-son, knew the village of Henoko. About $14,000,000 will be initially spent in the construction of the camp in the Easley Range area in Kushi-son. So Henoko is mushrooming rapidly like other boom towns; in 1955 its population was only 500, but by 1956 it was 7 times this. There are movie theaters, hotels, restaurants, and these and other constructions will be increasing more in the future at the rate of about 15 to 20 a day.

Before the construction boom the village people worked in the fields and mountains cutting the fire wood, construction lumber, charcoal wood and cultivating the virgin soil for the pineapple and tea plantations. Their yearly income was ¥80,000. But now most of its people have abandoned their fields and are employed by one of the construction companies as salaried men.

Kushi
Kannon-
do
Located on the primary road of Highway 13, just south of Kushi Village, it is not clear when this was erected. In olden times the prince of Tomigushuku, the local master of Kushi, went to China, and he became very ill. He prayed to the Buddha's statue every day that he might recover from his illness. When he was well again he brought the statue to Shuri for erecting a temple around it. But there were many temples in Shuri, so he could not erect one there. So he brought the statue to Kushi and erected a temple for it in this village.

1. War Monument of Oganiku
2. Dai-koku Tunnel.
3. Kaganzu Shrine.
4. Okuma Village.
5. Hentona Village.
6. Trans-Island Road.
7. Zajiki Village.
8. Zatsumu Tunnel.
9. Hedo Uehara Dam.
10. Kayauchi-Banta.

Northern Okinawa

This tour starts from the northern village of Ogimi-son, about 48 miles north of Sukiran. It goes to the northernmost village of Hedo from which can be seen, far off the shore, a small island which is one of the Amami group of islands which belong to Kagoshima Prefecture, Japan. Along the route, the tourist is impressed by the tombs facing the sea. Most of them are in groups like small villages and some of them are centuries old. You will also notice the stacks of faggots for firewood or the larger piles of construction timber. The people who live in the northern areas are largely farmers, so the cutting of firewoods and construction lumbers is an off-season occupation for them. They are not always cutting timber like professional woodcutters; they do this when they are free from their farms during the growing seasons. At certain times, you may see an entire family working at tying faggots or cutting timber, the husbands sawing the trunks, the women chopping and tying.

Ogimi-son — Composed of 16 small villages, and located on Highway 1, it has a population of 7,648 in 1,722 families and an area of about 17,847,000 *tsubo*. Ten percent of its main area, about 1,860,000 *tsubo*, is cultivated land. Most of the people are farmers; but there was insufficient arable land to support all of the inhabitants, so a number of the young people work away from home in southern Okinawa. Ogimi is famous for its banana cloth. This is made in a factory located in Kijoka Village on Highway 1, just before Okuma Village is reached. There the housewives' weaving group may be seen making textiles in the old manner. Producing more than their own personal clothing needs, the excess materials are sent to various retailers on the island. The group meets every day in the week with the exception of Sunday.

War
Monument
of
Oganiku

This is located on the east side of the village of Oganiku on Highway 1 about 50 miles north of Sukiran. The monument was erected in February 1958 with contributions collected from the villagers. The lettering thereon says: "We regard with respect and affection the people who sacrificed their lives for the country in war, and wish all people in the world to live in peace forever." There is also a list of sixty names of men of Oganiku who were killed in action during World War II.

Dai-koku
Tunnel

The Dai-koku Tunnel is about 52 miles north of Sukiran. Highway 1 passes through it just south of Okuma Village. The name Dai-koku is derived from the names of the two villages which it connects. The first word of the name *dai* (*dai* and *o* are represented by the same character in Japanese) is the first letter of Ogimi-son, and *koku* (same Japanese character as *kuni*) is the first letter of Kunigami-son. The tunnel was built in 1917; it is the second longest on Okinawa being 106 feet long, 14 feet wide, and 11 feet high.

Kunigami-
son

Composed of 20 small villages and comprising all the area north of Dai-koku tunnel, this is the largest and most northern *son* of Okinawa. Its area is over 18 square kilometers; it has a population, at

WAR MONUMENT OF OGANIKU

the present time, of 14,262 in 2,329 families; but about 3,000 of its people work away from home in southern Okinawa. Kunigami is a mountainous area which boasts 26 rivers; the highest mountain on Okinawa, Mt. Yonaha, which is 503 meters high, is located in this area.

Kaganzu Shrine
This is located in front of the Voice of America transmitter site in Okuma Village. It is dedicated to the Village-Protecting-God of Kaganzu Village. The new building was erected in August, 1958, with contributions collected from the villagers.

Okuma Village
Located on the highway a distance of about 57 miles north of Sukiran, Okuma was the capital

community of the village of Kunigami for the 182 years from 1732 to 1914. The triangular plain which borders the highway is called "Okuma Rice Paddy" and produces the largest quantity of rice grown at any single site on Okinawa. On the hill to the west stands the shrine of the "god of earth" which is worshipped by the villagers as the "god of farming". On the eastern hill there is a temple at the top of a flight of 53 steps. The people call this Kongorie Hill and they say the temple was erected about the same time as the one in Kin Village by the Japanese priest, Niisho. Many cherry trees are planted around the temple, so it is a beautiful place to visit in season and see the cherry blossoms. From the top of the hill, there is a very attractive view over the whole of Okuma Village, the Voice of America site, Okuma Rest Center, and the green rice paddies interspersed with colorful radio towers.

Hentona Village   Highway 1 passes through Hentona Village about one mile north of Okuma. Hentona is the present capital community of Kunigami-son; and a police station, a fisheries school, and several commercial firms are located in this village. The resident population is small, being only about 1200; but is the hub of government and private affairs for the scattered rural areas of Kunigami. There is a small bus terminal connecting the agrarian north with the industrial south. From Hentona to Nago, busses run every twenty-five minutes; but from Hentona to Hedo Village, at the northern tip of Okinawa, the busses run only twice a day. However, commercial trucks travel north of Hentona more frequently, bringing in fresh vegetables, purchased by the United States in 1958 for troops in Korea. These vegetables are grown on the farms of Kunigami around

SHRINE TO THE EARTH GOD

Hentona Village. A tempting assortment of radishes, cabbage, tomatoes, and other produce may be seen in the stalls of Hentona Village in season.

On the west side of the Hentona Village Office which is at the foot of a hill, the village-protecting-god shrine is located, and in front of the shrine is a kindergarten for the Hentona children. In an interview, the kindergarten teacher stated that, inside the shrine, there is a great natural cave which is large enough to accommodate the entire population of the village. During the last war, the cave was used as a shelter and is credited with saving the lives of the village people.

Hentona is famous for the Okinawan musical folk play,

Ie-shima Hando-gwa, a love story about a young girl of
Hentona named Hando-gwa and Kana, the son of the headman
of Ie-shima. Hando-gwa and her mother found the young
man, ill from exposure and drifting in his disabled boat, on
the shores of Hentona. He had set out from Ie-shima to buy
flowering cotton bolls. (The Hentona area, at that time, made
a prosperous industry out of exporting its home-grown cotton.)

Hando-gwa and her mother took the young man to their
home and nursed him back to health. The two young people
fell in love and were engaged. But at that time, the "loving
engagement" was unusual in Okinawa; all marriages were
arranged by parents. So the romance excited the curiosity of
the village people who felt no good could come from this viola-
tion of tradition. They watched the young man with suspi-
cion; and one day Hando-gwa's cousin, Machi-gwa, came to
her saying that the man had gone back to Ie-shima. Hando-
gwa refused to believe this telling her cousin that she and
Kana had sworn to the god that they would love each other
forever and would never separate. She added, "If I die, he
will die with me; and if he dies, I will die with him; so he
would not go to Ie-shima without telling me." Machi-gwa
replied that promises and oaths were just words used to
deceive and took her to the seashore where she showed her
Kana, sailing away toward Ie-shima. Hando-gwa then realized that her man had left Hentona, but she refused to believe
he had willfully deserted her.

So, early next morning, she went with her cousin to where
the ferry boat for Ie-shima was anchored on the Hentona
shore. Machi-gwa told the boatman how Hando-gwa had
cried all night, yearning for the chance to see Kana and ask
for some explanation from him. She asked the boatman to

SHRINE AT HENTONA

take them to Ie-shima for this purpose. The boatman shared
the common opinion that Hando-gwa's romance would be
ill-fated and refused to take them. He did not want to be
a part of any misfortune which might come to Hando-gwa
if Kana refused to receive her. But the anxiety he saw in
Hando-gwa's face and Machi-gwa's pleading touched him and
he agreed to ferry them to Ie-shima.

When they reached Ie-shima, Hando-gwa went alone to
Kana's house. He was not at home, but she knelt on the
mat before his father and told why she had come. The
father was very angry and told her that she could not be
engaged to Kana as he already had a wife on Ie-shima. He

kicked her crouching shoulders and told her to leave his house. Just then Kana came home from the office and his father asked him if he knew the girl. Kana was unmoved by the pitiful figure of the girl who had saved his life. He told his father he had never seen her before and did not even know her name. Hando-gwa implored him to tell his father the truth about them, reminding him that he not only knew her name, but had called it tenderly a hundred times a day when he was at Hentona. But Kana insisted he did not know her, and his father turned her roughly out of the house. Hando-gwa realized that the animal mind which Kana had shown could never appreciate the loving words she had come to say to him; and she decided that he should be punished for the treatment she had received and the dishonor which would come to her family through her.

The boatman, disturbed because she was so long returning, went to look for her and found her sitting on the road weeping. She told him what had happened at Kana's house. The boatman was angry that her tenderness to Kana in his illness had been repaid with such treatment and he said he would kill the young man. But Hando-gwa refused to let him stain his hands with blood for her. She assured the boatman that she was alright and told him that his words of sympathy to her were a fit souvenir for departing to another world. The boatman was astonished at the suggestion that she might kill herself. But she assured him that she would not die as long as the man who had betrayed her lived. Then she gave him a package containing a kimono which she had woven for Kana in the hope of seeing his smiling face when he received it. (In those days most Okinawan girls had their own looms on which they wove their kimonos. Very often, with tender affection, they would weave a kimono as a gift for their loved ones. So there are many folk songs about young girls weaving kimonos or towels as tokens of love.) Presenting the kimono to the boatman, Hando-gwa told him that this labor of love was all she had with which to reward his kindness. She then told him she would go to Gusuku Hill (the high peak on Ie-shima which can be seen from Okinawa) to cool her aching heart. She asked him to wait for her at his boat.

The boatman accepted the kimono and told her to be sure to return to the boat before sunset. She promised to do this, forcing a smile to hide her sorrow. Then she went to the top of the hill and, kneeling toward Hentona, asked her mother to forgive her for losing her heart to a strange traveller and for dying here in a strange place. Then she untied her hair and took out the 5-foot long *irege* (a circular rat on which the hair was done up) and used the artificial hair as a rope with which to hang herself. When she did not return at sunset, the boatman and her cousin, Machi-gwa, went in search of her. They found her body hanging by the *irege* and buried her on the east side of the hill, "from which you can see Hentona and not worry about departing to another world."

Hando-gwa fulfilled her promise not to die as long as Kana lived. Her ghost returned to plague him day and night until he became a very sick man. One night he asked his wife to bring him a cup of water; when he started to drink, it was suddenly turned into human blood. He sent his wife for another cup and the same thing happened to it. He was very surprised and frightened. Looking about him, he discovered Hando-gwa's ghost standing in front of his wife. So he went to the *toko-no-ma* and got his sword with which he started cutting down Hando-gwa's ghost. But then he heard his wife scream and saw her body fall to the floor. Realizing that the ghost of Hando-gwa had transformed itself into his wife and made him a murderer, Kana turned his sword upon himself.

Thus ends a true love story of a girl of olden times. The site of her house is to the southeast of the Hentona Village office; however nothing remains of this old romance but a few foundation stones.

The Trans-Island Road   This road connects the villages of Yona, on the East China Sea, and Ada, on the Pacific Ocean, in Kunigami district. The construction of the road was begun in December, 1951 with a five-year program of GRI industrial promotion funds to the amount of 10,000,000 yen. The construction of this road required five years because the route lay across a watershed which is 500 meters high. The road was opened to traffic in October, 1956. Before the construction of this road, if there was an emergency call in the village of Ada on the Pacific side, the people had to go laboriously over a precipitous mountain path to the village of Yona and then by bus to Hentona. Bicycles could be used on sections of the mountain path; but even so, it was a slow route to assistance. So when the road was opened and vehicular traffic over the mountain made possible, most of the people said, "We begin to see the light like a day's dawn." So they named the bridge between two mountain crests on its route "Yoake Bashi" (Bridge of Daybreak).

Zajiki   There is a village too small to be shown on many
          maps; it is just south of Sate Village. But its
seashore has been perpetuated in memory in the folk play,
Madan Bashi. It was to Zajiki Village that the husband
of the woman, Chira, whose life was sacrificed to build the
Madan Bridge in southern Okinawa, brought his infant
daughter. She grew up in Zajiki and it was on Zajiki Beach
that the young lord from Shuri whose father had ordered her
mother's death, found and fell in love with her. The play,
Madan Bashi is part of the repertoire of all Okinawan Actors'
Groups; but the recent trend to movie theaters has deprived
them of many places where these folk dramas were previously
performed.

Zatsumu   This tunnel is a pass on Highway 1 between
Tunnel   the villages of Uka and Ginama, a distance of
          about 66 miles north of Sukiran. It was con-
structed over a period of 4 years with industrial promotion
funds of Okinawa Prefecture. It was completed in August
1936 and is the longest tunnel on Okinawa: 172 feet long, 12
feet wide, and 15 feet high.

Hedo   The road going to this dam located in the northern-
Uehara   most mountain of Okinawa about 350 feet above
Dam   sea level is at the southeast end of the village of
          Ginama and climbs for about two miles from
Highway 1. This dam is the largest on Okinawa, its full
capacity for accumulating water being about 136,000,000
gallons. It moistens 240,000 tsubo of land. It was completed
in October 1956 following six years of labor. The cost of
construction was 27,000,000 yen six percent of which was

supplied by GRI, and four percent from local village funds.

Muduru-   About 42 years ago, there was no road over which
Michi   a person could carry anything up to the farming
            land on the east side of Ginama Village. So
people who had land on this side of the village, which is
50 meters high on the hill, had to climb up a steep cliff by
holding on to the trees and stumps on the mountainside. If
they met a person on the way who was coming down, they had
to make mutual concessions of the way to one another. Usually
the person coming up gave way to the one coming down. So
it was named "Muduru-Michi" which means "the Way of
Retracing One's Steps". In December 1911, Mr. Seiken Toyama, who came to his new post of Ginama Elementary School
Principal at the age of 26, could not remain a mere spectator
to students from Uehara Village on the east side of the cliff
struggling to school through the Muduru-Michi path. He
petitioned the village officers to build a road over the cliff.
They turned him down saying they had previously considered
building a road and found it not feasible. But the young
principal explained that, as the village grew there would be
more students in the future and the risk of attending school
by the Muduru-Michi path would increase. He convinced the
village people of the importance of the project and became a
leader in the construction of the new road to Uehara. The road
was completed on 3 November, 1913 and became a public
road to the villages of Uehara and Hedo. It is the present
Highway 1. A monument to Mr. Toyama is located on top
of the hill in honor of his meritorious service to the villagers
during his lifetime. The monument was unveiled in August

1958 and was built with labor donated by the Kokuba Construction Company, located in Naha.

Kayauchi-
Banta

On the east of a hill in Ginama Village is one of the eight most scenic spots on Okinawa.

The name "Kayauchi-Banta" may be translated as "Cliff from Which to Send-off Zebra Grass". The up-draft of wind from the bottom of the cliff is so strong that, when a bundle of heavy zebra grass is thrown from this high steep hill, it is lifted and dispersed like a mass of feathers. The pretty effect of the grass floating in the air is well known to all the people of Okinawa. So, when Kunigami district is mentioned, they immediately think of Kayauchi-Banta. The view from the top of the cliff is characteristic of the beauty of northern Okinawa; the highway snaking through the trees and past small settlements, Izena and Iheya Islands resting in the blue water and framed by the Motobu Peninsula. The commemorative stone on this high cliff was erected in January, 1957 as a tribute to the beauty of this spot.

Bibliography

Bond, Lucy—"About Okinawa". Star News Publishing Company, Okinawa, 1958. (English)

Kerr, George H.—"Okinawa, The History of an Island People". Charles E. Tuttle Company, Tokyo, 1958. (English)

Shinyashiki, Kohan—"Okinawa Folk Tales". Daily issues of the Okinawa Times. Okinawa Times Publishing Company, 1958. (Japanese)

Walker, Egbert H.—"Important Trees of the Ryukyus". US Civil Administration of the Ryukyus Islands, Naha, 1954. (English and Japanese)

World Almanac of 1946—"Chronology of the Battle of Okinawa". New York World Telegram, New York, 1947. (English)

Yonaguni, Zenzo—"Guide Book of New Okinawa". Okinawa Sightseeing Association, Naha, 1954. (English)

—— "Sin Kyodo Chizu, Gaho" ("Modern Okinawa Guide, Illustrated"). Okinawa Times Publishing Company, Naha, 1957. (Japanese with a modicum of English)

—— "Okinawa Today". Ryukyuan Review (weekly). Office of Information, Headquarters USARYIS, APO 331, 1958. (English)

—— "Visited Tourist Spots on Okinawa". Daily in the Okinawa Times. Okinawa Times Publishing Company, Naha, 1958. (Japanese)

—— "Inscriptions of the Cultural Property Commission of the Ryukyus'. Archives, 1949-58. (Japanese)

Yonaguni, Zenzo—Miscellaneous Articles on Okinawan History
    and Culture. The Morning Star Newspaper. Morning
    Star Publishing and Printing Company, Okinawa, 1957-
    58. (English)